# DAYLIGHT IN ARCHITECTURE

# DAYLIGHT IN ARCHITECTURE

**Benjamin H. Evans, AIA**

**Architectural Record Books**
**McGraw-Hill Book Company**

New York    St. Louis    San Francisco
Auckland    Bogotá    Hamburg
Johannesburg    London    Madrid
Mexico    Montreal    New Delhi
Panama    Paris    São Paulo
Singapore    Sydney    Tokyo    Toronto

# Architectural Record Books

The editor for this book was Patricia Markert.
The editing and production supervisor was Carol Frances.
The book was designed by Laura Ierardi.
It was set in Megaron Extended by Creative Graphics.
Printed and bound by Malloy Lithographing.


1234567890     890987654321

ISBN 0-07-019768-7

**Library of Congress Cataloging in Publication Data**

Evans, Benjamin H.
    Daylight in architecture.

    Includes bibliographical references.
    1. Architecture and solar radiation. I. Title.
NA2542.S6E9      720'.47      80-26066
ISBN 0-07-019768-7

Published by Architectural Record
McGraw-Hill Publications Company
1221 Avenue of the Americas
New York, NY 10020

# CONTENTS

# FOREWORD

This is a timely book. Ben Evans is helping us rediscover the sky. Daylighting has always been of major importance, but somehow during the 1960s, we forgot everything we knew about the art and science of daylighting. Cheap energy and air conditioning did us in.

The huge temples at Karnac, built 4000 years ago, were lighted by sun and sky through clerestories. The high windows of the great cathedrals advanced daylighting. Perhaps the zenith came in the 19th century, which produced the grand daylighted railroad stations, elegant hotels and mansions, commercial establishments, and of course, the Crystal Palace. Toplighting reigned. The 20th century has also produced some masters of daylighting. Among the most notable are Frank Lloyd Wright, Le Corbusier, and Louis Kahn. During the 1950s, the baby boom helped advance the science of daylighting as new schoolhouses began to appear throughout the United States. It was during this time that Ben Evans started experimenting to find out how natural light and wind behaved in and around buildings.

Then came the blackout period. The 1960s—a very formalistic period—snuffed out daylight. Either buildings had relatively few openings or they had all window walls, which is not a very clever way of achieving quality lighting.

Ben Evans remembers what architecture was like before this period. He had a hand in helping to discover in the research laboratory what every good architect wanted to know—how to use daylight creatively in buildings and at the same time satisfy the demands of the vision experts for good seeing conditions.

Evans has written a number of technical reports and articles over the years to help architects understand what can and can't be done with daylight. But in this book he shows a maturing understanding of the intuitive aspects of daylighting design that aren't resolved in the research laboratory. His illustrations and photographs demonstrate elements of good and bad design so that architects can easily understand what's significant and what isn't. In a very personalized approach, Ben combines his background in architecture and his consulting experience for some of the country's leading architectural firms, with his scientific and technical expertise to provide the reader with an approach to design for daylighting that should pay off.

**William W. Caudill, FAIA**
**April 1980**

# PREFACE

It is significant, rather than incidental, that people *like* daylight. If people like something, it stands to reason that they will view it as valuable and that when they have it they will be more content and more productive than when they don't have it. This simple fact, it seems, should assure that all built habitable spaces have an abundance of daylighting. But in recent years, it has not happened that way. When it is also discovered that an abundant supply of daylight can save money and improve the visual quality of the environment, daylighting of buildings should become the accepted rather than the exceptional practice. The purpose of this book is to help bring this about.

This book is intended for everyone who is involved in the design of a new building, but particularly for architects. If you are an architect, it will help you understand how to achieve good seeing conditions and a more human-satisfying environment. It will help you understand and justify these benefits to your client. If you are a prospective building owner, the book will help you understand that good daylighting will make your building more valuable and satisfying to those who will occupy it without increasing your long-term costs. If you are an illuminating engineer or lighting designer, this book will help you understand the potentials of daylighting as well as the architect's approach to its use. If you are a design student, this book will help enrich your design exercises by providing information and analyses not found elsewhere.

I have analysed those elements of good seeing conditions which I believe are relevant to the architect's design processes. I have been careful not to inundate the reader with all the scientific paraphernalia of the field which are mostly irrelevant to building design. The reader instead will find some thoughts, illustrated with analytical sketches, about the necessary and desirable integration of daylighting and other building design concerns, including another potential energy-saver—the use of natural air movement in lieu of air conditioning. There is a discussion of how buildings and their surroundings respond to daylight and some illustrated guidelines for effective design. I have attempted to provide a thought-provoking approach, not a stereotyped design formula. Included is a discussion about the nature of the skies from which daylight comes with some charts and tables for use in determining how much daylight will be available at your building site. There is a discussion of how to evaluate design alternatives through the use of simple scale-model studies while the design is still in the preliminary stages. Text and sketches illustrate how to build proper models, how to select and use lighting instruments in model studies, and how to conduct field tests under a real sky. The book does not deal with mathematical formulas or computer-based prediction techniques which are useful for analysis and evaluation of alternatives, but not for basic design. The reader will find a discussion of the potential energy/cost savings from the proper use of daylight that will help justify the daylight approach to design. Finally, there is an analysis of a series of case studies of buildings, illustrated with drawings and photographs, demonstrating those elements of design which contribute to and distract from good daylighting design.

## Acknowledgments

I have prepared this material in response to requests from students and colleagues for a descriptive treatise on the utilization of daylight in buildings as discussed in my graduate classes at Virginia Tech University. In my classes, I approach all subjects from the viewpoint of design—that is, the end product of all discussion and study is the production of design for the integrated, *total* environment. Exploration of more finite subjects, such as daylighting, energy optimization, etc., is viewed only as contributing to the *total* design process. Qualitative analysis always takes precedent over quantitative analysis, but only after the student has grasped a fundamental understanding of the value and shortcomings of the quantitative approach.

This book is a distillation of a 30-year collection of technical and research papers blended, like good whisky, with my own research, study, and experiences. I hope the brew has not gone to my head, but that it will be a stimulant to others. I am indebted to W. W. (Bill) Caudill, FAIA, for starting me on the road to research into daylighting when I was his student at Texas A&M and, more importantly, for his instilling in me the sense that research and daylight are only tools to help us create better architecture. I am also grateful to the late Bob H. Reed, colleague,

and for a period, leader of our architectural research team at A&M, for his patience with me and for teaching me the skills of inquiry. Growth always requires an antagonist, and for that I thank J. W. (Bill) Griffith, daylighting consultant and economist, who has so often laughed at some inept conclusion of my befuddled mind, but who has always been willing to set me on the right path. To William G. Wagner, AIA, my architectural critic and longtime friend, go my thanks for his guidance. Thanks go to Neil Carter, one of my graduate students, for preparing the background material for Chapter 7. Someday, if I'm lucky, I may be working for Neil. My thanks to faculty colleague Keith Hughes and to graduate student Cary Dunn for photographic advice and for processing my film. To the National Endowment for the Arts goes my appreciation for a grant that made much of the research behind this book feasible. To my sixth-grade English teacher, whose name I don't remember because she taught me nothing, I send my thanks. Writing with an easy and full grasp of literary skills could not be as much fun as the struggles I have been through. My special thanks go to my daughters Ann, Lynn, and Gail who provided the right amount of skepticism, and to my wife for her encouragement and spelling coaching. (She says I am the most creative speller she knows.) To you, Gwendolyn dear, go my thanks for the best life I could have found.

**B.H.E.**

# DAYLIGHT IN ARCHITECTURE

# 1

# INTRODUCTION

From the dawn of time until the widespread introduction of the fluorescent lamp during the post-World War II period, the sun was the predominant source of daytime light in buildings. It was far more available and effective than other sources, and it provided mankind with a continuing relationship with nature and the outdoors which were close to his origins. The introduction of daylight into buildings shaped structural concepts, stimulated product development, and, in general, influenced the form of architecture for the creation of some of our greatest buildings.

As the world struggled to get through the Great Depression prior to World War II, the predominant means for lighting buildings were windows, skylights, and a few incandescent lamps. If the lighting environment wasn't the greatest, people nevertheless accepted it for the most part and got along as best they could. The war propelled us into rapid technological development and raised the standards by which we measured adequateness of life. By the time the baby boom hit in the early 1950s, Americans had great expectations and every reason to believe that their children would realize untold benefits from the new age. Education was foremost on the list of priorities, resulting in a school building boom that lasted for 15 years, accompanied by the development of an intense demand for quality in the school program and environment. Nothing was too good for our children, and we were suddenly affluent enough to afford a new level of quality. If a little light had been enough before, now there must be a lot of light. Lighting, as one example, took on a new level of significance.

Architects began to explore ways to get plenty of "good quality" daylight into the schoolroom. Sawtooth roofs, skylights, clerestories, double- and triple-lighted rooms, tinted glass, and all sorts of techniques were tried in an effort to get the daylight to where it was thought to be needed. Much was learned about daylighting both in the field and in the research laboratories. At the Texas Engineering Experiment Station, where I was introduced to daylighting research in 1950 and where I participated in the development of an extensive environmental research laboratory, we worked with many architects in testing design concepts with simulated sky and sun. At Southern Methodist University, J. W. Griffith and his research associates tested full-scale buildings and models to develop the daylight calculation technique finally adopted by the Illuminating Engineering Society (IES). As a result of these and many other efforts, some very excellent daylighted school buildings were built and many still exist. The design of other types of buildings also was influenced by this experience. There were, of course, some failures along the way—perhaps more failures than successes—because neither scientists, architects, nor educators knew exactly what constituted good visibility in the classroom and because changing educational concepts placed new demands upon the classroom design almost yearly.

At the height of this building boom, along came the economical and efficient fluorescent lamp, offering the potential of lots of in-

FIGURE 1-1. Flexibility of space use is often necessary, leaving the architect with a dilemma about the type of lighting to provide.

expensive lighting and broad architectural flexibility. Its use quickly became widespread. For the remainder of the school boom, and the concurrent boom in all types of construction, electric lighting became the almost exclusive mode, and daylight was gradually forgotten.

With the availability of convenient and inexpensive luminaires and ample supplies of cheap electric energy, *quantity* of light quickly became the measure of quality. While scientists still toiled in their laboratories to gain new insights into the basics of good visibility, the selling of light quantity in the marketplace overshadowed their efforts, which were seldom noted, often misunderstood, and frequently misapplied. Those few voices in the wilderness who questioned the new practices were shouted down.

Then came what was probably one of the most sudden and dramatic changes in the history of the world—the energy crunch. With the realization that the fossil fuel energy reserve was rapidly being depleted and with the costs for that energy increasing almost daily, it was only natural that designers again began to look to daylight not only for ambient lighting, but for task lighting as well as a means of conserving energy.

There are those who claim that daylight should be used only for "effect" and windows only for view, leaving the production of task lighting to electric luminaires. This is a shortsighted view of what is possible and financially profitable. Architects seeking creative and functional designs, who understand the principles of daylighting, can and will find ways to use it effectively as others have in the past. The question is not whether daylight can be effectively used, but when, where, and how.

During the years between the daylight era of the mid-century and the energy crisis of the 1970s there was almost no advancement in knowledge or understanding in this country of the use of daylight in buildings. But with the current search for ways to save kilowatts, designers are once again beginning to focus on daylighting and on quality of visibility as potential energy-savers of significance. There are, however, some attendant problems. Few architects or lighting designers know very

much about how to use daylight effectively. Many do not understand the fundamentals of what constitutes quality seeing conditions, and few architects, engineers, and lighting designers understand the respective roles of their fellow professionals.

Many of the electric-lighting designers who are most informed about what constitutes quality lighting do not seem to understand the architect's primary goals in building design or some of the constraints within which he has to operate. Conversely, architects do not always understand that electric wire and technologically superior luminaires are not a substitute for good building design. The architect's goal is to design a *total* facility to achieve something akin to what Vitruvius called "commodity, firmness, and delight."

A total design is seldom optimal in all of these aspects and almost always involves a number of compromises. Design for acoustics must be coordinated with design for durability and cleanliness, for instance, resulting in a product that is of somewhat less quality than might be achieved if acoustics were the only concern. Thus, perfection in lighting may have to give way, to some degree, to quality in structure and mechanical equipment or to economic constraints.

There seems to be evidence that the general parameters of good lighting are known and that, given a set of architectural circumstances, designing a lighting system to produce a good visual environment can be done. One of the problems here is the lack of willingness or ability of the building owner-operator and/or architect to define specifically what visual tasks will occur at what locations and under what conditions for the total life of the building. Some clients may simply want to put off making a decision about lighting during the early stages of design because of what they consider more pressing concerns. It is up to the architect to insist on some concrete decisions early in the game in order to avoid problems that only have to be faced later, and often at the expense of increased costs and lowered quality of visual conditions.

Given specific criteria and objectives for the use of a space, the architect can design a facility that will be responsive to these criteria. For instance, if the client and the designers can describe a space, what is to occur in it, where persons will sit and work, and how much and what kind of light these persons should have, etc., the architect can produce a responsive lighting design. But architects seldom get this kind of specific direction. Clients frequently do not know specifically where the furniture will be placed or, if they can provide a furniture layout, where the individual pieces will be moved sometime in the future. Frequently, owners of speculative buildings may not even know who or what is to occupy their building spaces. This leaves the architect with a real dilemma with regard to lighting, acoustics, air conditioning, and so forth. How can the architect design for properly lighted tasks if he doesn't know what those tasks will be or where they will be done? The only answer to this particular dilemma is that the lighting system must also be flexible enough so that when the space is finally occupied, *someone* will be able to arrange for a satisfactory visual performance scheme. Having the options that go with flexibility probably will cost additional dollars. The client who is to get

FIGURE 1-2. People seldom approach their tasks from a predictable position.

quality lighting should be prepared to pay the initial price—it will be recovered tenfold over the life of the facility. Architects and illuminating engineers alike should understand that the client's demand for flexibility will place additional constraints on the building design, but, for the client, the demand may be quite reasonable and, often, absolutely necessary.

In addition to that kind of flexibility, there is also the problem, associated with visibility, of the occupant who cannot be "nailed down" to a specific spot. He turns and fidgets, walks around, slouches in his chair, holds his books or papers first one place, then another, and in general makes it difficult to place a luminaire, even the finest, where it will always provide the best light.

There are ways to deal with these circumstances, but, again, they are seldom simple or inexpensive. What all this leads to is the recommendation that the architect and lighting designer not be *overly* concerned with all the research reports, technical articles, and computer data which espouse finely tuned lighting systems and lighting levels that must meet someone's laboratory-developed criteria. The good architect has a finely tuned sense of intuition which, ideally, allows the total design to be seen in proper perspective. The architect, concerned with all of the parameters which constitute good design, exercises this conditioned intuition to achieve an acceptable whole design.

This is not to suggest that the architect should ignore scientific or experimental evidence. On the contrary. Intuition can only be effective if it is based on a thorough understanding of the fundamentals of good lighting (as well as other design parameters).

Since so little attention has lately been given to daylight and its accompanying solar heat contributions, there is considerable confusion not only about whether or not daylight can be effectively used for task lighting, but also about whether or not daylighting can save energy, and if so, how much. The answer to this, simply stated, is that daylight can be effectively used for a wide variety of purposes and, properly used, can conserve energy in most circumstances while at the same time adding

FIGURE 1-3. Louis Kahn's Kimbell Art Museum is a masterpiece of intuitive daylighting design, "where natural light is a light of mood."

measurably to people's satisfaction with, and appreciation of, their living and working environments. This is not to say that daylight can be used for every purpose nor that it should always be used for any purpose. Daylight is one of many tools at the designer's disposal and, if properly understood, can often provide the means to an effective end.

It is the phrase "properly used" which allows such statements to stand without immediate repudiation and which constitutes the basis for this book. How is daylight to be properly used?

# THE NEED FOR LIGHT

Certainly, light is necessary for people to see to accomplish specific tasks such as reading, writing, sewing, and so forth. But ==light also helps to define space through visual perception== (without light there would be no visual perception), ==and daylight has certain attributes which make its use in defining space, form, color, and texture particularly productive.==

Much has been said and written about vision and the effects of light on the seeing process. It will not all be reiterated here. However, it seems worthwhile to discuss some of the major factors in the seeing process that will be of immediate concern and value to the architect.

## SEEING THE TASK

==Visibility,== which is the state of being perceivable by the eye, is often thought to depend principally upon the amount of light on the object or task to be seen, and that *more* light on the object or task will make it *more* visible. To some degree this is true, but visibility also depends upon visual acuity (the ability to distinguish fine details), and contrast sensitivity (the ability to detect the presence of luminous, or brightness, differences). Both visual acuity and contrast sensitivity vary with task luminance (brightness), which is determined by the amount of incident light, where the incident light comes from, and the reflectivity of the task. A 1 percent loss in ==contrast== may require as much as a 15 percent increase in illumination to achieve equal visibility. To put it another way, you have to be able to see the contrast between the task and its immediate background. (You couldn't see the type on this page if there weren't contrast with the paper. You could see it better if the type were darker.) And the whole seeing process is dependent upon the physical state of a person's eyes!

But visual acuity is also a function of the ==size== of the task and the amount of ==time== available for viewing. If the task detail is large, it is easier to see. Large typeface is easier to see than small typeface. Fine detail is made easier to see if one can take more *time* in the process of looking. Tasks that are more critical in terms of time than those normally encountered might be inspecting a ball bearing on a fast assembly line or reading the label on a revolving phonograph record.

It is in the area of task size and contrast where considerable light and energy savings could occur, if clients would use ballpoint pens, for instance, rather than pencils, along with larger typewriter typeface and fresh ribbons, and if publishers of newspapers, magazines, and books would use larger typeface. If these conditions were met, a few footcandles of light might well suffice.

But clients aren't always willing or able to bring about these kinds of changes. As one whose eyes are failing with age, I look for books which are printed with large type because they are easier to read, but I buy books with small type because they are less expensive, and besides, you can't often find adult books with large type.

You will seldom find a children's book with the small type you see in this paragraph. Children are less familiar with the letter characters, and editors want the characters to be big enough so that the child doesn't have to spend extra time trying to see. I believe you will agree, unless you have unusually good eyes, that this small type is more difficult to read than the type used elsewhere in this book.

However, given enough time, the average person will be able to make out the small type if the quality of illumination on the book is reasonably adequate. But what if the quality is not adequate?

FIGURE 2-1. As the illumination increases, visibility also increases.

FIGURE 2-2. As the contrast increases, visibility also increases.

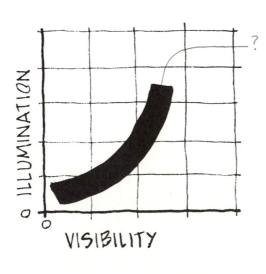

ENOUGH LIGHT TO SEE

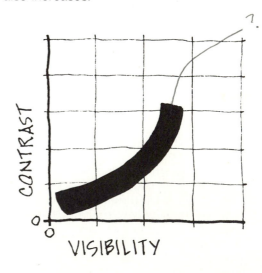

ENOUGH CONTRAST TO SEE

## Veiling Reflections and Contrast

The measure of quality of light on the book or similar task is very much related to contrast sensitivity which, as already noted, is a function of the brightness differences between immediate task and background (type on paper). If the available light strikes the task surface at an inappropriate angle, and the light bounces off the task (dark type) into the eye, the contrast between the task and surround may be reduced and, hence, visibility will be reduced. This condition is called a "veiling reflection"—the task is "veiled" from view because of the way the light strikes it and is reflected to the eye.

This angle from which the light strikes the task and is reflected to the eye is often called the "mirror angle." The mirrored angle effect is easily observed by placing a mirror, or other shiny surface, over the task and looking for light sources reflected in the shiny surface. If you can see the light sources or bright surfaces in the room reflected from the mirror or task area, you have a veiling reflection condition that can reduce contrast and make seeing more difficult.

Take the front page of any newspaper and place a piece of plastic wrap over it. Newspapers typically offer a range of contrast qualities from very poor to fair and a range of sizes of typeface. Move the newspaper around. Lean back and put your feet on the desk. Hold the newspaper in your lap. Place it on your desk. Move it from left to right. It will be very surprising if in any one or all of these positions you do not observe light sources reflected in the plastic. Notice how these reflections reduce your ability to read the underlying newspaper print easily. This is the phenomenon which is most often associated with poor seeing conditions. *It is the principal failure of typical ceiling-grid electric lighting systems*. And, as you can see, it would be difficult to locate light fixtures on the ceiling so that no veiling reflections exist when you move your newspaper around.

However, if you sit so that the light comes

FIGURE 2-3. As the task size increases, the required illumination decreases.

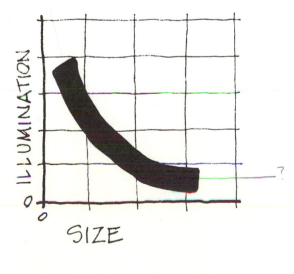

SIZE

ENOUGH **SIZE** TO SEE

FIGURE 2-4. As the time available for seeing increases, the required illumination decreases.

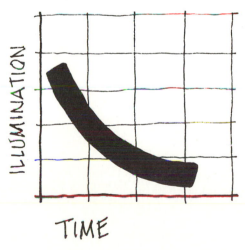

TIME

ENOUGH **TIME** TO SEE

FIGURE 2-5. VEILING REFLECTIONS ARE THE RESULT OF INCIDENT LIGHT WHICH COMES FROM THE "MIRROR ANGLE," REDUCING THE TASK CONTRAST AND OBSCURING DETAILS.

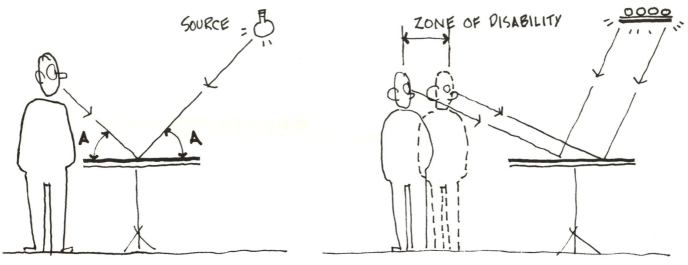

THE ANGLE OF THE **INCIDENT** LIGHT WILL **EQUAL** THE ANGLE OF THE **REFLECTED** LIGHT

A **LARGE** AREA LIGHT SOURCE PRODUCES A LARGER ZONE OF **DISABILITY**

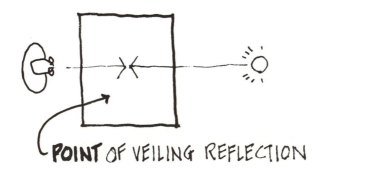

**POINT** OF VEILING REFLECTION

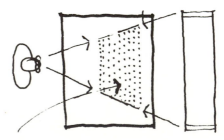

**AREA** OF VEILING REFLECTIONS

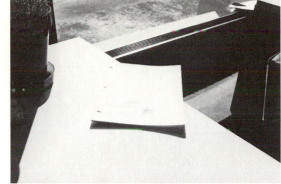

FIGURE 2-6. The contrast of the task (left) is reduced by veiling reflections (right), making it more difficult to see clearly.

over your shoulder and there are no lights directly in front of you, it is not likely that any veiling reflections will be seen on the plastic covering the newspaper page. The effect being sought, however unconsciously, is the elimination of veiling reflections and excessive brightnesses within the field of view.

Now sit with the window on your left (or right) and have someone turn off all electric lights in the room. The chances are, even though the footcandles of light will be reduced, you will be able to see the newspaper under the plastic sheet better than when the lights were on.

This is a clear demonstration that quantity of illumination is not the total answer to good lighting. It should also demonstrate the additional potential for saving electric energy in a building "properly designed" for use of daylight.

There are ways, of course, to construct electric lighting systems so as to eliminate or reduce these veiling reflections. In general, they involve spreading the source of light over a large area (indirect lighting on the ceiling and walls) so that the light delivered to the task will come from a large source of low brightness and the percentage of light from the mirrored angle will be relatively small. Luminaires can also be selected with lenses that direct the light and

minimize the area of the room in which veiling reflections will occur.

The use of windows for daylight does not eliminate the possibility of veiling reflections. It does, however, reduce the possibilities over a much wider area of the interior space for a wider variety of task locations. If one sits facing a window, with his task in

FIGURE 2-7. Indirect lighting which spreads the light over a large area of ceiling and walls helps to moderate veiling reflections on the task.

FIGURE 2-8. With the eyes adapted to exterior brightnesses, surfaces in shadow appear dark, areas inside the building, very dark.

between, veiling reflections will certainly be more likely. Also, excessive brightness differences will be more likely, and visibility will be reduced.

Designers of school buildings in the 1950s and 1960s sought to respond to educational concepts requiring flexibility of space use (where it was not always desirable to locate students facing away from the window wall) by eliminating or reducing windows and turning to ceiling-mounted fluorescent luminaires. The result was the substitution of one problem for another, but because of the quantity and uniformity of light level provided by electric light, it was mistakenly perceived as the preferable system.

## The Perception of Brightness

We have been taught to think about lighting principally in terms of footcandles. But you can't see a footcandle. You only see an object that is *lighted* with footcandles when the light is reflected to the eye. What we see is *brightness,* which is a function of the amount of light falling on the surface and the reflectivity of the surface (ability to reflect light). Technically speaking, luminance is the measure (in footlamberts) of that phenomenon, and brightness is what we *perceive.* It would be much better in architectural design if we could specify perceived surface brightnesses rather than footcandle levels. This would allow the designer to take into consideration all the ramifications of the intangibles such as aesthetics and psychological reactions as well as visual function.

The human visual system is capable of responding to an extremely wide range of surface luminance. An object perceived in the night may have a brightness of only a few thousandths of its brightness under direct sun. It is the control of these relative brightnesses that will determine whether or not any lighting system is successful. But our subjective perception of relative brightnesses is, to a large extent, based on the eye's ability to adapt.

We see objects clearly and distinctly when in the bright sunshine, where the illumination level might be 12,000 footcandles and the luminance of, say, a sidewalk is 5500 footlamberts. If we enter a dark theater from this sunshine, where the illumination level may be less than 1 foot-candle and the luminance of a floor less than 1 footlambert, we become almost totally blind. However, after we've been in the theater for 20 or 30 minutes, we find that we can probably see quite well and may wonder where all the light came from. Our eyes have simply adapted from one condition to the second. Conversely, when we leave the theater and return to the sunshine, another period of rapid (sometimes seconds) adaptation will take place.

Similarly, our eyes go through more subtle adaptation stages as we move about and through variously lighted spaces. The sequence of photos here illustrates how the apparent brightnesses of surfaces and objects change as the eye's adaptation level changes.

The appearance of bright surfaces adjacent to shadowed surfaces depends on the eye's adaptation level as well as the luminances. Raise the adaptation and the shadows look darker. Lower the adaptation and the shadows look brighter. Hopkinson states, "thus a surface with a luminance of 100 footlamberts has an apparent brightness of 100 when one's eye is adapted to 100 footlamberts, but the same surface would have an apparent brightness of 230 when one's eye was adapted to 10 footlamberts."[1]

Patterns of luminous intensity can be *measured* and expressed in footlambert levels, or luminous ratios, but these measurements do not indicate the *apparent* brightnesses due to the eye's ability to adapt. Researchers at Pratt Institute found no correlation between measured luminance levels (footlamberts) and observed brightnesses in a number of surveyed buildings.[2] Even measured luminance then, does not provide a very good indication of the perceived brightness which is modified by the surrounding conditions and the state of the eyes. The perceived relationships between various brightnesses provide the base for proper lighting design.

Competing brightnesses have long been recognized as undesirable for good visibility conditions. The ideal visual environment has often been described as a field of constant and uniform brightness. Of course, no such environment exists outside the labo-

FIGURE 2-9.   Once inside the building, the eyes adapt to lower levels of brightness, and the areas that appeared very dark from outside are now quite visible.

FIGURE 2-10.   Looking back toward the exterior from the inside, the exterior surfaces appear to be excessively bright, whereas the interior is easily visible.

FIGURE 2-11.   The brightness of objects outside the window competes with the brightness of the book for our attention, reducing the perceived strength of the desired signal.

ratory, nor would people be very satisfied in such an atmosphere. Brightness differences add meaning and beauty. But excess brightness differences in the field of one's view is another matter. A bright light fixture or brightly lighted sky when viewed simultaneously with a modestly lighted task, such as a book, reduces the visibility of the type.

Lam states that "Bright sources which are not the intended focus of attention cause the eye to adapt to a high average brightness level, reducing the perceived strength and quality of the desired signal. We react defensively when such sources cannot be excluded from the field of vision."[3]

The loss of visibility caused by such excessive brightness ratios decreases as the competing brightness is removed from the center of vision or as it approaches the brightness of areas in the immediate field of view. Ideally then, brightness ratios should range from 1:1 between task and the surround with increase allowed away from the central field of view, to a ratio that should not exceed about 1:20. The recommended surrounding brightness ratios should not be confused with the necessity for contrast (or brightness difference) between the immediate task (pencil writing, printing, etc.) and the task background (e.g., paper).

What all this means for the architect is that lighting systems, whether daylight, electric light, or a combination of both, should avoid, to the extent possible: first, producing veiling reflections on task areas; and second, excessive or competing luminance ratios when they are to be in the field of view. These criteria are not always easy to achieve, but when they are considered from the outset of a building design, they are reasonable goals.

## Equivalent Sphere Illumination
Several years ago, the IES adopted the concept of Equivalent Sphere Illumination (ESI) as a method for incorporating some element of *quality* into illumination level measurements. As has been pointed out, illumination on a task may provide good visibility or it may create veiling reflections which impair visibility. ESI provides some

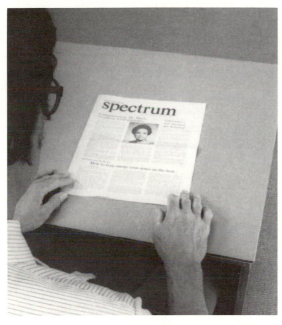

FIGURE 2-12.   With a brightness ratio between task and immediate surround of 1:2, we have no difficulty in seeing the task.

FIGURE 2-13.   With a brightness ratio between task and surround of 1:10, we still have no difficulty in seeing the task.

FIGURE 2-14.   With a brightness ratio between task and window of 1:100, we cannot see the task at all because our eyes have adapted to the brighter areas.

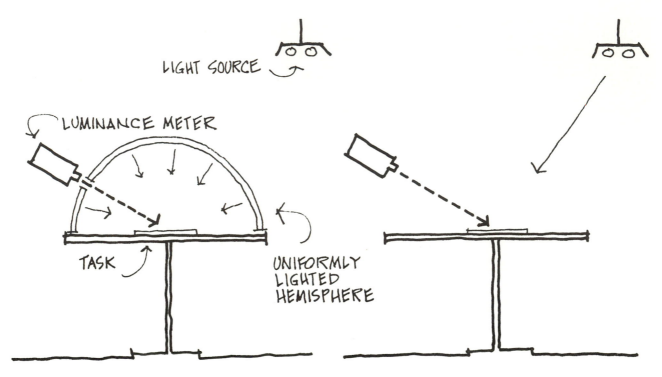

LIGHT SOURCE

LUMINANCE METER

TASK

UNIFORMLY
LIGHTED
HEMISPHERE

FIGURE 2-15. ESI COMPARES SPHERE LIGHTING WITH THE **REAL** SITUATION.

measure of the *visibility* of a given lighting condition. ESI is a metric for the measurement of *visibility potential.* Sphere lighting (the perfectly diffuse lighting of an integrating sphere) is used as a reference so that a given amount of its light always produces the same amount of visibility. The ESI of a visual task at a particular point in a real lighting situation, viewed from a specific direction, is that level of lighting produced by a photometric sphere, centered around the task, that makes the task as visible as it is in the real lighting situation. That is, the visibility of the same specific task in the real lighting situation is *equivalent* to that produced by some level of sphere illumination. An illumination level of 50 raw footcandles (as measured by a conventional light meter) on a task whose contrast is reduced by veiling reflections, may be the equivalent of 25 ESI. The ESI (measured with a complicated ESI meter) provides an indication

that the visibility *under that particular lighting situation* and *from that particular direction* is less than the 50 raw footcandles would indicate. In other words, because of the veiling reflections, much of the light reaching the task in this particular situation is less than beneficial to our seeing.

ESI is useful as a concept. It does not, however, provide a very practical tool for designers in a "real world" building situation, except under very specific circumstances where the location of tasks and the sources of light can be firmly prescribed. Designers will find that a thorough understanding of the fundamentals of good lighting and good visibility will provide the mechanism for adequately evaluating lighting designs.

**Quantity of Illumination**
Once there is an understanding of the qualitative criteria of veiling reflections and

brightness perception, the question of *how much* light we need becomes somewhat easier to deal with. Obviously, there must be enough light provided in building spaces for occupants to see what they want to see. But who is to say what is enough and, wouldn't "more be better?"

For many years, we have all been accustomed to "single-number" recommendations for illumination levels for typical rooms, as in "70 footcandles on the horizontal desk level for a classroom." These single-number recommendations have usually been plucked out of an Illumination Engineering Society (IES) table, since the IES is just about the only source for such data in North America. The IES, including its constituent Illuminating Engineering Research Institute, is the one organization to continually and systematically support research into vision and lighting and to foster a continuing dialogue about quantity and quality. Whereas there have been questions raised about the validity of IES's consensus single-number values, the research upon which these recommendations has been based remains the best that is available to us, and those who would criticize are hard pressed to provide more reliable answers. The inherent problem with any single-number, light-level recommendation is that it either fails to take into consideration, or overemphasizes, that there are usually a variety of tasks and lighting demands involved in most spaces. We usually assume, for instance, that children in a classroom should be able to read light pencil handwriting, so we specify that the lighting system produce the required number of footcandles for that task at desk height throughout the classroom. But the issue is more complex than this. The process fails to consider the combined needs of varying visual tasks in the same room—such as reading a textbook with large type, a blackboard, a map on the wall; sewing, drafting, or building with blocks. It also fails to consider how much light there should be on a wall, floor, or step, or how to produce a mood or desired atmosphere. These tasks may take place simultaneously or sequentially in the same "typical" classroom, but they do not require the same amount of lighting. Nor does this single-number sys-

tem respond very well to problems associated with less than normal eyesight or the inadequacies of sight that occur as a result of age.

In 1972, the IES published its most recent single-number illumination recommendations based on a *weighted average* of data and assumptions about user eyesight, age, task demand, and so forth, and these recommendations were published as Table 9–80 in the IES *Handbook of Lighting,* 5th Edition. Since then, besides some new research findings, the nation has become entangled in a complex pattern of social rebellion, rising power costs, and increasing building construction costs, all of which have brought about some changes in societal values and goals. Where before we wanted as much light as we could get, now we want as little as we need.

In 1977, the IES began working toward a recommended system that would be based on "actual task performance objectives," while recognizing that there still are many voids in our knowledge of the processes of seeing and of task performance objectives. In June 1979, the IES adopted a new system which now constitutes the basic policy regarding procedures for determining task illuminance recommendations.[4]

The new system tries to avoid specifying the level of illumination needed in building spaces by general-use category (e.g., 75 footcandles for a classroom, which was based on certain assumptions). The new system puts the burden on the designers to make their own assumptions, but it provides guidance based, as much as possible, on recent research findings.

The system involves two tables. The first (Table 2-1) covers recommended illumination ranges for a variety of categories of tasks, while the second (Table 2-2) provides the weighting factors to be applied to the range of illumination values chosen from Table 2-1.

In Table 2-1, categories "A," "B," and "C" provide a range of illuminances to cover the entire area of an interior space. For instance, in a circulation space such as a hotel lobby or office building corridor, the visual task (seeing where to walk) remains constant with time and throughout the space, and an illumination-level range is

TABLE 2-1.  Illuminance Recommended for Use
in Selecting Values for Interior Lighting Design*

| Category | Range of Illuminances Maintained in Service in Lux (Footcandles) | Type of Activity |
|---|---|---|
| **General lighting throughout room** | | |
| A | 20-30-50 (2-3-5) | Public areas with dark surroundings |
| B | 50-75-100 (5-7.5-10) | Simple orientation for short temporary visits |
| C | 100-150-200 (10-15-20) | Working spaces where visual tasks are only occasionally performed |
| **Illuminance on task** | | |
| D | 200-300-500 (20-30-50) | Performance of visual tasks of high contrast or large size: reading printed material, typed originals, handwriting in ink and good xerography; rough bench and machine work; ordinary inspection; rough assembly |
| E | 500-700-1000 (50-70-100) | Performance of visual tasks of medium contrast or small size: reading medium pencil handwriting, poorly printed or reproduced material; medium bench and machine work; difficult inspection; medium assembly |
| F | 1000-1500-2000 (100-150-200) | Performance of visual tasks of low contrast or very small size: reading handwriting in hard pencil on poor-quality paper and very poorly reproduced material; highly difficult inspection |
| **Illuminance on task, obtained by a combination of general and local (supplementary) lighting** | | |
| G | 2000-3000-5000 (200-300-500) | Performance of visual tasks of low contrast and very small size over a prolonged period: fine assembly; very difficult inspection; fine bench and machine work |
| H | 5000-7500-10,000 (500-750-1000) | Performance of very prolonged and exacting visual tasks: the most difficult inspection; extra-fine bench and machine work; extra-fine assembly |
| I | 10,000-15,000-20,000 (1000-1500-2000) | Performance of very special visual tasks of extremely low contrast and small size: e.g., surgical procedures |

*Adapted from Table 1.2, *Guide on Interior Lighting*, Publication CIE No. 29 (TC4.1), 1975.

recommended (the range being 5-7.5-10 footcandles).

Categories "D," "E," and "F" generally involve tasks that remain relatively fixed at one location in most work situations and, therefore, should be applied only to the appropriate task area, recognizing that there may be several different tasks in a single space or room. In addition, the IES also recommends that 20 footcandles be regarded as the minimum illumination on the horizontal surface at work height for the general "non-task" portions of the rooms where continual visual work is performed.

Categories "G," "H," and "I" are for extremely difficult tasks. The lighting system for these categories requires very careful analysis.

Table 2-2 provides the weighting factors used to select a specific design illumination level from the range provided in Table 2-1. These weighting factors take into consideration the age of the users, the reflectance of the task background (e.g., paper, chalkboard), and the degree of demand for speed and accuracy—all factors readily identified by research as significant variables.

As an example, for reading a medium-pencil task on an 80 percent reflectance paper by a group of teenagers in a classroom where speed and accuracy are not particularly important the recommendation would be 50 footcandles, which is derived as follows:

- From Table 2-1, the range of illuminances for reading a medium-pencil task is Category "E," and the range is 50-75-100 footcandles.
- From Table 2-2, for teenagers (below 40 years) the weighting factor is −1.
- From Table 2-2, since speed and accuracy are not important, the weighting factor is another −1.
- From Table 2-2, for a reflectance of task background greater than 70 percent, the weighting factor is another −1.
- From Table 2-1, with a total weighting factor of −3, the lower number of the range (50 footcandles) is selected.

There are subtleties and refinements in the new IES system that are not covered in this brief summary. The complete system with all of its refinements is available in various IES publications.

What all this means to designers is that they are now in a position to make more specific decisions than in the past and that they now have significant guidelines to handle a variety of tasks and conditions even when they are in a single space. The IES recommends:

. . . that the designer, through client/occupant/designer interaction, establish the tasks of prime importance, with an appropriate hierarchy of other tasks. Similarly, the time duration of each task, worker ages, expected task performance, and task characteristics must be determined. If all or many of the tasks require similar lighting quantities, then the designer might design the room lighting system to meet one representative task, and this would also meet the majority of the other task requirements. If, however, the tasks vary considerably in their lighting requirements, then the designer should consider multiple level systems, unique work layouts,

variable control systems, or some combination of systems in order to accommodate a number of tasks of varying visual requirements in an energy-conscious and economic manner.

Further, what this means for designers is that they will now be in a better position to evaluate for their clients the trade-offs which can be made, such as the cost of higher illumination levels measured against the value of fewer visual mistakes made in performing the task.

Nowhere in the new IES system is there any mention of daylight or of other types of light sources. The system is not dependent on source. Keep in mind also that this system is for selecting task performance *levels* only and deals only minimally with quality. The other factors which also govern quality must be understood by the designer before these recommended levels can be applied effectively.

TABLE 2-2. Weighting Factors to be Considered in Selecting Specific Illuminance within the Ranges of Values for each Category in Table 2-1*

| Task and worker characteristics | WEIGHT | | |
|---|---|---|---|
| | −1 | 0 | +1 |
| Workers' ages | Under 40 | 40-55 | Over 55 |
| Speed and/or accuracy** | Not important | Important | Critical |
| Reflectance of task background | Greater than 70% | 30-70% | Less than 30% |

*Weighting factors are to be determined based on worker and task information. When the algebraic sum of the weighting factors is −3 or −2, use the lowest value in the illuminance ranges D through I at Table 2-1; when −1 to +1, use the middle value; and when +2 or +3, use the highest value.

**In determining whether speed and/or accuracy is not important, important, or critical, the following questions need to be answered: What are the time limitations? How important is it to perform the task rapidly? Will errors produce an unsafe condition or product? Will errors reduce productivity and be costly? For example, in reading for leisure there are no time limitations and it is not important to read rapidly. Errors will not be costly and will not be related to safety. Thus, speed and/or accuracy is not important. If however, prescription notes are to be read by a pharmacist, accuracy is critical because errors could produce unsafe conditions, and time is important for customer relations.

## BIOLOGICAL NEEDS

Since recorded history, people have attached special significance to the sun and its resulting daylight. It has been the subject of worship and countless other considerations. Humanity has evolved and endured under the special energy of the sun. When the fluorescent lamp took over the lighting of interiors, and window sizes were reduced and often eliminated, there was a hue and cry from many about the degeneration of the human environment. As a result, numerous studies have been conducted to determine whether or not there are any detrimental effects from the absence of daylight and windows. The psychological aspects of these studies were summarized in Collins' *Windows and People: A Literature Survey.* A general conclusion that can be drawn from this study is that significant psychological advantages and disadvantages to windowless buildings have only been substantiated through occupant preference studies.

On the other hand, some studies on the physical aspects of light have resulted in specific, although limited, conclusions with regard to the biological effects of light on animals and humans. Bissonnette and others have shown that migration and sexual cycles are more dependent on light than on temperature. Wurtman points out that Dutch and Japanese farmers often have exposed birds to extra light in the autumn of the year in order to induce singing among songbirds and to increase egg production in ducks and chickens.[6] Bissonnette notes that increased night lighting induces cottontail rabbits to undergo extra sexual activity in the winter. There are many more such pieces of isolated evidence that indicate light has specific influences other than that normally associated with vision.

### Effects of Daylight on the Human Body

But what specifically of daylight? Ott states that "Life on this earth has developed in response to the full spectrum of natural sunlight, and variations in the wavelength distribution by artificial light sources, or distortion of the wavelength distribution of sunlight filtered through glass, seems to result in variations for normal growth development in both plants and animals."[7]

Ultraviolet radiation is, we know, essential to human welfare. It prevents rickets, keeps the skin in a healthy condition, is responsible for the production of vitamin D, destroys germs, and affects certain necessary chemical changes in the body. When the body is exposed to ultraviolet rays, there is a dilation of the capillaries of the skin. Blood pressure falls slightly. In addition to a feeling of well-being, there is a quickening of the pulse rate and appetite, plus a stimulation of energetic activity. Work output may actually be increased. Of course, overexposure can cause damage such as wrinkles or even malignant tumors of the skin.

In the natural environment, there is a plentiful supply of ultraviolet even in areas of high pollution, and most of us who spend any time outdoors receive a reasonable dose. But if we spend most of the daylight hours inside, the amount may not be sufficient. In the artificial environment we receive almost no health-giving ultraviolet. Incandescent light is almost completely lacking in ultraviolet. Ordinary fluorescent tubes aren't much better, although at least one manufacturer is currently producing a fluorescent tube which includes some ultraviolet light in its output. Some mercury lamp sources are rich in ultraviolet light, but sufficiently deficient in other qualities so that they are seldom used indoors. The question then is, "to what extent can and should ultraviolet and other aspects of natural light be utilized for favorable biological response in humans?" There seems to be no complete and definitive answer to this question, but there is certainly a risk in *not* exposing people to certain bands of wavelength.

Faber Birren writes, ". . . if man hazards extermination through lack of oxygen, atomic radiation, water and air pollution, the disruption of nature, he also may find himself in trouble if he does not comprehend the secrets of sunlight and adapt them to his purpose in the establishment of his environments."[8]

### Uniformity of Stimulus

Uniformity of almost anything becomes monotonous when we are exposed to it for a long enough period. Even the best perfume eventually becomes just a "smell."

Put a fine painting on the wall in front of your desk and stare at it long enough without interruption, and soon it will seem commonplace rather than a great painting. The human organism is not adapted to steady stimuli or to the complete lack of stimuli. The statement made earlier that excessive brightness ratios in the field of view should be avoided suggests that the best visual conditions are achieved in a uniform environment, but lack of change is inconsistent with the natural capabilities and tendencies of people. It is here that the constantly changing nature of daylight automatically and naturally responds to the need of the body and mind for a change of stimuli or mood.

The human organism is in a constant state of flux, its functions rising and falling, depending on the stimulus to which it is exposed, and sometimes changing even without stimulus. The body responds to steady state conditions by changing itself. The pupil of the eye will expand and contract even with exposure to a constant and uniform brightness. The brightness will appear to fluctuate. But if the monotony is long continued, the body's *ability* to respond to stimuli will gradually deteriorate until subtle changes cannot be perceived at all. People require changing stimuli to remain sensitive and alert. Seated, with our attention on some task for a while, we will instinctively seek change and relief by looking out the window; or in the absence of a window, across the room, up at the ceiling, or at anything else that will provide the necessary natural relief—lighting a cigarette, cleaning a pipe, or trimming fingernails. The muscles of the eye become fatigued when vision is concentrated too long, and looking out the window and concentrating on distant objects will provide the relieving exercise.

Comfort and agreeableness are related to moderate changes. Monotony may cause distress, but so may overstimulation. The sudden appearance of a beam of direct sunshine on the task may provide momentary change and relief, but if it remains, will soon cause visual fatigue and stress. Both uniformity and excessive contrasts are to be avoided. Monotony may lead to visual efficiency, but it will also lead to emotional fatigue. Excessive contrasts may

provide emotional acceptance, but also may impair good visual performance. An architect once put a very dark red wall in a schoolroom design that I had recommended have uniformly white walls. I wanted what science seemed to suggest would provide good visibility. He wanted excitement and visual relief. He was right. The students were excited by the red wall and never complained about its visual restrictiveness, if there was any.

The trick in building lighting design is to find a way to provide reasonably subdued surface-brightness variations while at the same time providing some visual flexibility and stimuli (Figure 2–16). The proper introduction of daylight into the environment is the simplest and most effective way to provide these valuable variations.

## Excessive Brightnesses and Windows

Excessive brightness *ratios* in the field of view generally result in poor visibility. One should not have to try to read a brightly lighted book when it is surrounded by very dark or exceptionally bright surfaces or sources of light. In this regard, the window and the view it provides of the bright sky or brightly lighted outdoor objects can be a serious offender. If, however, the light intensity and surface brightnesses inside the room are sufficiently high, the ratio of brightnesses between sky and task may not be excessive, and therefore may be tolerable. For instance, if the brightness of the visible cloudy sky is 6000 footlamberts, a sheet of white paper having a reflectance of 80 percent must be illuminated with 377 footcandles to provide a brightness ratio between the sky and task of 20:1. Such a footcandle level is far in excess of anything recommended for any ordinary task.

The usual response to this dilemma is for designers to use tinted glass in the windows to reduce the visible brightness of the sky. But this has the corresponding effect of reducing the available daylight and the footcandle level inside the building, thus also reducing the brightness ratio and compounding the problem. Typically, a glass with a transmission factor of about 10 percent might be used to reduce the visible sky brightness from 8000 to 800 footlamberts, correspondingly reducing the

FIGURE 2-16.   The lobby of the Regency Hotel in
Dallas. Welton Becket, architect.

available interior daylighting by 90 percent. Thus the needed interior illumination would be about 64 footcandles not now available from the windows, but easily supplied by electric light if plenty of cheap electric light were available.

The essential result of this process is that the windows become simple "vision strips" whose only function is to allow a view out. Recent developments in "high-performance" glasses allow for a high percentage of reflected heat and light with a moderate amount of visible transmission. But in most cases, the amount of usable daylight that reaches the interior through these high-performance glasses is moderate, useful only for a minimum of ambient lighting, and does not alleviate the need for electric light.

It is for this reason that I have formerly not recommended the use of tinted glasses. But architects in the southern and southwestern parts of the country particularly, have insisted on its use, instinctively feeling that people cannot tolerate a view of those excessively bright skies from indoors, and they may well be right. Ferree and Rand maintained years ago that the presence of a bright source of light or other surface of high brightness in the field of view produces a blinding effect through a phenomenon called irradiation, which seems to confuse and blur seeing in direct relation to the intensity of the source. The presence of high brightnesses in the field of view disturbs the ability of the eye to adjust, rapidly leading to fatigue in the muscles of eye adjustment and the loss of ability to sustain the precision of adjustment needed for clear seeing. This may be the reason so many people wear sunglasses which reduce not only exposure to bright surfaces and sources, but also reduce desired visibility of objects.

In situations, then, where excessively bright outdoor surfaces or sources can be viewed from inside, the use of tinted glasses to reduce brightness and still allow vision out may be a very acceptable solution—for vision—but not for daylighting of interiors. Light or daylight for interiors will have to come from elsewhere. Thus the two highly desirable normal window functions of lighting and vision may have to be separated

FIGURE 2-17.  Windows with darkly tinted glass contribute little daylight to the interior and are used essentially as "vision strips."

and resolved with different solutions, the techniques of which will be discussed later.

**Orientation.**  The need for the human body to be able to relate to its natural surroundings both mentally and physically is well established. Aviators who lose contact with the horizon and the exterior surroundings in adverse weather are subject to vertigo and must use instruments to maintain level flight. Vertigo of this kind can be a physical problem in the sense that, through disruption of the inner ear balancing mechanism, the aviator loses all sense of up and down; and it can be a mental problem in the sense that the aviator cannot logically sense when flight is level. But every aviator will support the claim that if one has a good sense of orientation before one flies into a fog bank, one will be in much better condition to maintain, however briefly, some semblance of direction and balance.

For those who are accustomed to outdoor living, such as the farmer, fisherman, hiker, or hunter, not having a general sense of orientation is tantamount to getting lost and/or failing in the task at hand.

FIGURE 2-18. This movable ramp to transport passengers from plane to lobby has no visual reference to the exterior and provides passengers little indication of which way is up.

Passengers on a ship are much more likely to experience sea sickness if they are below deck with no contact with the horizon. The movement of the ship upsets the equilibrium of the inner ear and ultimately results in nausea. A similar, though usually less noticeable, effect occurs when people are inside a building with uneven floors or walls having no view of the exterior. People may stumble on gentle ramps not realizing the slope is different from the floor. They may bump their heads on sloping walls. A classic example is the movable catwalk or ramp in many airports which transports passengers from plane to lounge. These ramps stretch out to accommodate the different airplane heights and locations at the loading dock and permit passengers to walk up or down on their transitional journey. Unfortunately, most of these ramps are windowless and are decorated inside as if they were built on level ground. Thus the passenger is disoriented and only a casual observation is needed to witness their stumbling feet.

The techniques for overcoming such problems in buildings include providing clearly defined vertical and horizontal surfaces such as wainscots, striped wallpaper, hanging paintings, and so forth. For airline ramps, a simple window allowing vision of the horizon or exterior would be sufficient.

A related kind of disorientation occurs when people are completely cut off from their natural environment and lose track of time and weather conditions. Humans have some kind of internal mechanism which keeps track of time—the rhythm of day and night and the seasons. Most women can confirm the fact that the "internal clock" regulates their menstrual cycle, and that dramatic changes of environment can alter that inner clock. Travelers who traverse the time zones know the effects of "jet lag" and the need to allow the body time to adjust to a new time cycle. People are subconsciously frustrated when they are not able to sense what is happening with the weather outside nor to have some sense of time.

During World War II, a gigantic airplane fabrication plant was constructed in Texas. There were no windows, although plenty of electric light was provided. Before many months of occupation, employees had set up a telephone watch with secretaries in the outer administrative offices to report periodically on the exterior climate. In another such plant where the windows were translucent, and therefore provided no view, the glass panels were smashed and, as quickly as they were repaired, smashed again, presumably to provide employees some sense of contact with the exterior and changing weather.

**Sunshine.** One of the strongest elements in the establishment of a sense of orientation and well-being is the presence of direct sunshine in buildings. The evidence of a desire for some direct sunshine is strong, although it may be strongest for residents of northern latitudes where the duration and intensity of available sunshine is more limited. Observations by Richards[9] and Morgan[10] suggest that people in South Africa and Israel tend to avoid sunshine. These preferences are most likely related to availability. Those in the northern climates, where there tend to be fewer sunny days, have an almost overwhelming desire to go south. Those in the more temperate southern climates may find the sun commonplace, uncomfortable, or monotonous. However, experience indicates that the southerner who is moved to the northern latitudes will too soon come to miss the presence of sunshine.

Ne'eman and Longmore reported that among the occupants of schools, houses, offices, and hospitals questioned, 42, 90, 73, and 90 percent respectively wanted some sunshine in their environment. The difference in preferences, the authors con-

cluded, may be related to the availability of shading devices for control of glare and heat gain.[11]

To some extent, the desire for sunshine in buildings is related to the task at hand. Certainly, the presence of direct sunshine inside can interfere with good seeing because of the excessive brightness associated with it. However, if the task is more casual, the presence of sunshine may be much more desirable.

In the United States, large circulation areas in hotels and shopping centers, lighted with skylights and glass walls, have become very popular. Direct sunshine enters these voluminous spaces in varying degrees. These hotels with their central atriums and abundance of daylight and

FIGURE 2-19. Direct sunlight on the task can make seeing very difficult because of the excessive brightness.

FIGURE 2-20. Multistory atria and circulation areas in shopping malls and hotels with daylight and direct sun have become very popular.

sunshine have become major attractions to conventioneers as well as curious passers-by. Skaters on the ice rink in the Galleria in Houston are treated to sunshine winter and summer (Figure 2–22). Where there is this sense of carnival and excitement, people seem to love the "outdoor" lighting and atmosphere.

While there is minimal scientific evidence to support claims regarding human need for orientation and contact with the surrounding climate, surveys by Ruys[12], Somner[13], and others have established the definite preference for windows and a view out by office and factory workers. Wells reported that in a study of office workers, 69 percent believed that daylight provided a better quality of illumination for office work than "artificial" light.[14] Wilson reports on a study of hospital rooms that patients in windowless rooms experienced an increase in stress levels and exhibited a doubling of post-operative delirium cases.[15] On the other hand, Pritchard suggested that among factory workers in windowless spaces, the level of complaint might be inversely related to the amount of money the employee was making.[16] Studies by Hollister in 1946 of the first underground factories in Sweden indicated that initially, employees reported headaches and fatigue, but that over a period of time complaints tended to cease.[17] Many an architectural design has endured because of the adaptability of people!

In the April 1978 issue of the *AIA Journal,* a number of "underground" buildings were presented along with various comments by the architects about their design goals. The primary stimulation for the underground approach was energy conservation through thermal loss reduction, but a remarkable number of comments were made about the need for relating the interior to the exterior environment, and the buildings all showed a remarkable sensitivity to the desire for sunshine, openness, and view of the exterior. So much so, that one could argue whether or not these buildings should properly be classified as "underground."

The evidence indicates an overwhelming preference for windows which let in daylight and provide some view to the outside. The degree of the preference seems to be

FIGURE 2-21. Where there is a sense of carnival, people seem to love the "outdoor" lighting. The Galleria in Houston. S.I. Morris, architects.

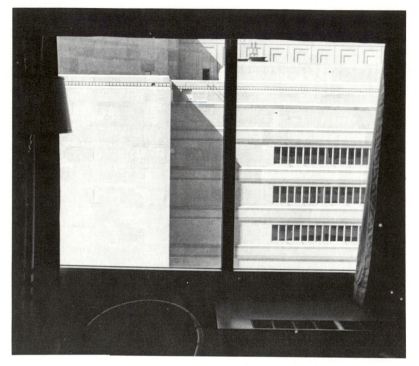

FIGURE 2-22. Even with a poor view, a window provides information content about the weather.

rooted in the amount of time spent in a space, the type of task performed, and the persons' expectations based on cultural and geographical background.

**View.** Although the techniques for getting daylight into interior spaces are not necessarily directly related to view, they very often are related, and a few comments about the value of the window from the standpoint of view also are in order.

Any leasor of building space will confirm the fact that tenants are willing to pay more for office space next to the windows than for windowless spaces, and that the corner spaces with windows on two sides will bring the highest premium. A multitude of comprehensive research projects about window views would not provide more convincing proof that we humans need the window. However, in 1967, Markus noted, ". . . it is not surprising to find virtually no work to establish an optimum performance of windows with regard to their fundamental function—acting as visual apertures enabling building occupiers to remain linked to the external world in some way."[18]

Nevertheless, ample research substantiates our intuitive sense of what the view should provide. The information content of the view constitutes the most significant factor. Simulate a brick wall a few feet outside your office window, light it with hidden electric lights, and you will not find its information-giving properties very valuable. However, if your office window were constructed a few feet away from another building with the between-space extending all the way to the roof and the street, enough daylight would filter through to your window to give you quite a bit of information about your environment. You could sense the changing weather conditions and keep track of time, even if in a very limited way.

The exterior view area may be divided into three content areas: the sky (upward), the horizon (level), and the ground (downward). Each of these divisions provides some of the information needed for the biological satisfaction already discussed. The view of the sky provides information about the time of day and weather conditions, thereby helping us to maintain our proper biological cycles, and it provides a varying light exposure which helps to reduce monotony. The view of the horizon provides that stabilizing and comforting inner feeling so that we know which way is up and which way is down and that we are securely tied to the good earth. The view of the ground helps to tie us with the activities of the world outside and often to let us know something of what is going on outdoors. Over all, the more complex the view and the more frequent the changes, the more likely will be our satisfaction with it.

Asked what kind of view they prefer, most people will express a desire for the natural landscape. But when subjects have been exposed to a variety of possible views, as by Ludlow in 1972, they were not satisfied with static landscaping no matter how beautiful.[19] They preferred a complex structural organization in the view containing a balance of synthetic and natural things with some element of movement, change, and surprise involved.

An office in a multistory building in Washington, D.C., has a window facing down into a semi-interior courtyard, very nicely landscaped. Surprisingly, even after very short occupancy, the view becomes monotonous, except when the secretaries occupy the courtyard during their lunch hour. The view to Pennsylvania Avenue from an office on the street side of the building—with traffic, ambulances, police cars, pedestrians, drug store, and theater—is preferable to that of the courtyard. Admittedly, for concentrated work the occupant can avoid distractions and excess brightnesses in the field of view by looking the other way.

The leasor of building space will confirm that large expanses of glass seem to be desirable from the standpoint of view, but that clients who are willing to pay the premium rental price for lots of glass are often few and far between. While large windows may be desirable, people's basic need for a view seems to be satisfied with even relatively small windows, the ideal minimum being somewhere between 20 and 30 percent of the view wall area (Keighley).[20] While vertical openings are more effective in letting in daylight and provide greater information content about time and weather, people generally find narrow, vertical openings less desirable than a wider and shorter opening. A basically horizontal shape seems to provide the most desirable view. Nevertheless, when circumstances prevent the use of large, horizontal openings, any opening is better than none, and often the basic time-weather information can be had through the use of narrow slits and skylights.

**Brightness Gradients.** Daylighting generally produces a gradation of light on surfaces and objects that biologically is "natural" to us. The normal result of daylight is the "standard" against which our minds measure all things seen, probably because of a lifetime of association with daylight. In that sense, daylight provides some advantages over light from other sources. With electric lights located in the ceiling and elsewhere, we must be very careful about the surface brightness gradients produced. Uneven brightnesses on a uniformly flat surface will make that surface appear uneven.

FIGURE 2-23. The exterior view may be divided into three information content areas; the sky, the horizon, and the ground.

FIGURE 2-24. Vertical windows provide a limited range of visual information content.

FIGURE 2-25. Surfaces are perceived as evenly lighted as long as the change of brightness is at a constant rate.

Hurvich and Jameson state that the brightness will appear more or less uniform throughout an area in which the luminance gradient is constant.[21] Lam argues that "surfaces are perceived as continuous and evenly lighted as long as the luminance gradients (the ratio of change of the luminance, not the absolute luminance) seem natural and appropriate for the shape of the surface."[22] The wall or ceiling lighted from a window will appear to have a uniform brightness even though the light on the wall at the window is more intense than away from the window, assuming, of course, that the window is adjacent to the wall surface. A wall surface that is separated from the glass area by a significant opaque area in the window wall will have a low-brightness area next to the window wall, and therefore will appear uneven. More will be said later about the technique for avoiding this.

However, if the continuity of a flat surface is broken by a natural joint, change in material, or structural element such as a beam or column, the two areas may be perceived as uniform even though the brightness is non-uniform over the entire area. Spaces that provide a "natural" break between portions of surfaces daylighted and electrically lighted, will tend to seem more natural.

**Color Constancy.** Daylight is often thought to be "natural" light and all other sources "artificial" light. In the strict sense of the word, there is no such thing as artificial light—there are only natural and man-made sources. Our so-called "natural light" is an arbitrary thing. Each source of light has its own color spectrum or wavelengths, and the color spectrum of daylight, as we see it, changes during the day. Humans know all sorts of light, from orange-pink dawn and dusk, to yellow sunlight, to white or bluish skylight, and they are endowed with a special biological faculty known as "color constancy" to accept them all as "natural."

Generally, the human eye and mind can accept colors of objects as natural even with a "non-white" light source, incandescent for instance, if the color spectrum is not too different from normal daylight. Some designers are now using sodium light sources indoors, claiming that people get used to the predominantly yellow light. Whether people can happily adapt to a light that is so different from "natural" remains to be seen. Undoubtedly, it will depend very much on the environment and the task to be performed. But if different types of sources are used in the same space, the difference in appearance of various colored surfaces will be objectionable. However, they may be quite acceptable if they are used to highlight different types of objects and surfaces. If a wall, for instance, is lighted by daylight, an incandescent downlight on that wall will appear to be noticeably yellow. But if a picture on that wall is lighted by the incandescent, the mind's eye will accept the mixture of the two light sources with ease.

Illuminating engineers generally accept, as a standard white light, the particular spectral characteristics of the north sky on a sunny day in June at Washington, D.C. The lighting industry has thereupon tried to

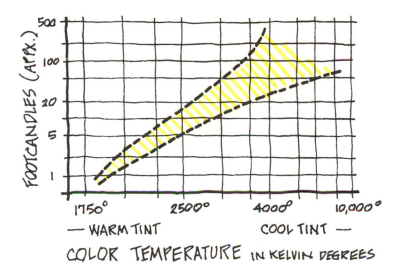

FOOTCANDLES (Appx.)

500  100  20  5  1

1750°   2500°   4000°   10,000°

— WARM TINT          COOL TINT —

COLOR TEMPERATURE IN KELVIN DEGREES

FIGURE 2-26. In Kruithof's Principle, the colors of surfaces will have a "natural" appearance only if the color of the light source is warm at low levels of intensity, and cooler at high levels of intensity. In the chart above, the region of natural appearance lies within the white space between the two curves.

duplicate this light in electric sources. But humans are seldom exposed to the kind of light described for Washington. The orange and red tints of dawn and dusk are "natural light" too, as are the white sunlight and bluishness of a cloudy day. The differences in the color of daylight and electric sources of light for buildings only become a concern when we must experience them both at the same time, as we invariably must. Suffice it to say that electric light sources should be selected to properly mix with daylight in buildings where daylight is to be admitted in significant quantities.

Pertinent here, however, are the findings of Kruithof, which show that to achieve a normal appearance of object colors, different colors in a light source will be required, depending on the intensity of illumination present.[23] In low levels of light (under 30 footcandles), object and surface colors will appear normal when the light source is somewhat pink, orange, or yellow. At higher levels of illumination, a "normal" appearance for object colors will be found with cooler light that is more like sunlight and skylight at noon. For daylighted buildings, this suggests the use of electric lamps with different light spectrums for daytime and nighttime use.

## SUMMARY

Light is needed if we are to see, but the quality of that light is more significant than its quantity. The context within which light illuminates objects in the environment and the way in which those objects are perceived is equally important. What people think they see is as important as what some designer wants them to see. Basic needs of the human organism are sometimes more important in the long run than the immediate need for good seeing conditions. In building design, consideration of all these criteria simultaneously is the architect's principal task, and these concerns must be integrated with other factors of the physical environment.

# DAYLIGHTING IN RELATION TO OTHER DESIGN CONSIDERATIONS

Daylight cannot, of course, be considered as an entity entirely unto itself without consideration for other design parameters in buildings. The architect seeks to produce a holistic environment, appropriate in total context and as correct as possible in each of its systems and parts. But each of its systems and parts are unlikely to be perfect, since each must function in respect to often conflicting demands. Thus, a building becomes a series of compromises in which often its separate parts are not entirely ideal. Marble facing in the hotel lobby may be considered more important than the accompanying acoustical dilemma, or the cost of air handlers more consequential than control of air speed.

Daylighting, therefore, must be measured against effects on the total building, and all of its separate parts and daylight must work in cooperation with other elements rather than against them. In many respects, this is not difficult, but, as with most elements of a building, the method and extent to which daylight is to be used must be considered from the very outset of building programming and design. Calling in a con-

FIGURE 3-1. INTEGRATE DAYLIGHT WITH OTHER DESIGN CONCERNS.

- SOLAR ENERGY
- DAYLIGHTING
- NATURAL AIR FLOW
- ACOUSTICS

sultant after the preliminary design has been completed and demanding that a ''daylighting design'' be applied will not produce very satisfactory results. At best, it can only confirm or deny that the daylighting design will produce some specific result. The effective design of a building to use daylight properly must begin in the conceptual stage. Daylight must be a part of that creative process which attempts intuitively to integrate all the important functional and intangible factors into a workable product. In this chapter, we will consider the relationships between daylight and several other of those closely allied parameters which are also a part of the whole.

## ELECTRIC LIGHTING

Electric lighting, and in particular, the fluorescent lamp, has had a greater effect upon the form of buildings than almost any other modern innovation. Electric lighting has been and is an exceedingly valuable contribution to the welfare and efficiency of society. Its use, fortunately, will continue (perhaps abated) in spite of shortages of energy. The question before us is not whether to use electric light or daylight, but when and where to use each and how to get the most from each.

There are significant differences in subjective impressions of quality and character of typical daylighted and electrically lighted interiors. The sources are generally in different planes, so that the flow of light from them has a different dominant direction. They provide light, generally, of different spectral composition. Daylight varies in intensity and composition, whereas electric light does not. Daylight is transmitted; electric light is emitted. One comes with the dawn and disappears with the night; the other may be interrupted by power shortages or equipment failure. Use of one may allow exterior noise to accompany it from outside to inside; the other generates noise (from the ballasts). A fenestration which admits daylight can provide a view to the exterior. Electric lights can be positioned and even moved so as to put light where it is most needed. Fenestrations can be used to admit, along with daylight, air to be used for cooling. Electric fixtures can be integrated with the air-conditioning system for simplification of equipment and to carry off unwanted heat. Both electric luminaires and daylight openings (presumably with glass) must be cleaned for best performance. The same criteria for the production of good quality lighting applies to both sources. The lighting of interiors should be accomplished with the proper combination of both sources, taking advantage of what each has to offer.

Current figures indicate that of the total energy consumed by commercial buildings, as much as 40 to 50 percent of it is in the operation of the electric lights. As the price of electricity continues to increase, as it most assuredly will for the foreseeable future, there is sufficient incentive for reducing as much use of electric light as is humanly possible, consistent, of course, with the programmatic objectives of the building's owner.

## Switching

The electric lighting systems in most existing buildings have been designed without real regard for the contribution of daylight from windows. Windows have been used primarily for view, with the daylight contribution considered an extra or fringe benefit with no quantifiable value. The primary exceptions to this are residences, schools, and skylighted warehouses, in which value was considered, if not quantified. The result is that electric lights throughout the country are turned on in the morning and left burning throughout the day, regardless of daylight availability. One of the simplest solutions to this wasteful practice is to provide switches for the electric lights, particularly those next to the windows, so that they can be switched off when there is a sufficient quantity of daylight. Of course, people will not necessarily use the switches just because they are provided, unless there is some particular incentive for them to do so. Some organizations have found sufficient incentive in strong leadership from the management.

On-off switching can be handled on a circuit-by-circuit basis, on a fixture-by-fixture basis, through individual ballasts within a single fixture, or with the use of multilevel ballasts. The latter options, although involving more expensive switching and control systems, provide effective

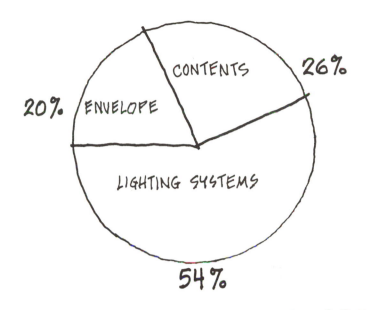

FIGURE 3-2. ANNUAL ENERGY CONSUMPTION FOR A TYPICAL OFFICE BUILDING (1960-1970)

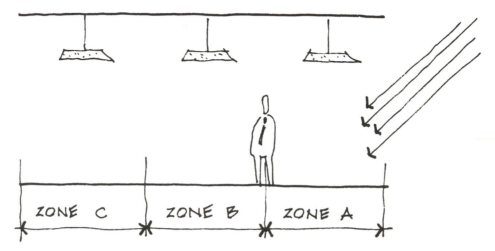

FIGURE 3-3.   DAYLIGHT ALLOWS
DIMMING OR SWITCHING OF ELECTRIC
LIGHT BY ZONE TO CONSERVE ENERGY.

multilevel footcandle capability, without some of the undesirable user response to on-off systems.

But in a typical office building, the perimeter floor area that may effectively be lighted by daylight (penetrating into the space typically about 15 to 20 feet) may amount to as much as 50 to 60 percent of the total floor space and presumably about that percentage of luminaires normally used for electric lighting. If this percentage of luminaires could be switched off, even for a portion of the day, the energy savings would be truly significant. In the daylighted Shell Oil buildings in Houston, individual switches were located next to the working spaces so they would be convenient to the occupant's touch. Sufficient daylight is anticipated to make their use unnecessary most of the time.

To eliminate dependency upon occupants to turn switches on and off, automatic devices are available to do the chore. Luminaires can be connected to light-sensing devices that will deactivate the switches when the available daylight reaches a prescribed level. One, two, and even three banks of perimeter electric lights, or banks of individual tubes, can be controlled by these light-sensing devices so that rows of luminaires are automatically illuminated as the available daylight decreases. Conversely, luminaires are switched off as the daylight availability increases.

But switching has the disadvantage of calling attention to the change. Almost everyone will be aware of the immediate contrast if the electric lights are switched on or off. No matter how satisfactory, desirable, or superior the changed condition is, it will probably require some interruption of thought and an adjustment period—for the mind if not the eye—that many people will find objectionable. Dimming systems are coming on the market that will prompt activation of the luminaire lamps on a gradual basis. A new generation of solid-state electronic ballasts promises to provide dimming at only moderate increased cost. The electronic ballast, just coming onto the market as this book goes to press, also provides energy savings as compared to conventional core ballasts.

## Compatibility

Experience conditions our minds and bodies to accept the characteristics of daylight as the norm. It is the standard against which other sources of light are compared, even though, as previously mentioned, its characteristics tend to change with the time of day and season. We each have a "color memory" that helps us to see a white surface as white, even though the light striking it changes in color output from noon to evening. Thus, electric lighting systems in buildings must achieve a degree of compatibility with the daylight that is to be admitted—compatibility in terms of color, direction, and general effect.

With the wide variety of lamps now available, color compatibility is not difficult to achieve. Fluorescent tubes sufficiently close to daylight in spectrum are available so that the casual observer will be unaware of the differences. Even incandescent lamps, historically rich in red and yellow emission, are now being made with "daylight" characteristics. Metal halide lamps also produce relatively good white light, as do some of the improved mercury lamps. Sodium vapor lamps, which have become more popular lately because of their high output of lumens per watt, have a distinctly yellow color and render many surfaces and objects, especially human complexion, a very unfavorable color. Sodium lamps are generally acceptable on highways, in parking lots, and on walkways, but are not likely to be very acceptable where people have to look at each other in their light. People viewing sodium vapor lamps simultaneously with buildings whose interiors are lighted with cool fluorescent light may find the juxtaposition disagreeable.

Still, there are valid reasons for sometimes using lamps with a particular spectral output. The reddish-yellow output of typical incandescent or deluxe warm white fluorescent lamps, for instance, is considered beneficial next to mirrors in bathrooms and make-up areas. Researchers have found that the human memory of true complexion color is substantially on the pinkish side.[1] People seem to prefer complexion tints that are ruddier than the actual tone of their own flesh. This might suggest that the cooler tint of daylight should not be used in bathrooms and make-up areas where warm light is desired. On the other hand, the desirability of using daylight may be sufficient to offset any potential problems with color. There are techniques for avoiding the discomfort of conflicting and different light sources used in close proximity.

If two distinct light sources, one warm in tone and the other cool, are directed on a white wall, part of the wall will appear yellowish and part will appear bluish. The juxtapositional result will be undesirable. However, if the wall under the warm light source is painted some color (say, orange) and the surface under the cool light source left white, the differences may not be "color pure," but the human eye and mind will perceive the two areas as distinctly different and therefore compatible. In the first instance, the two light sources produce a varicolored wall which the observer perceives to be unnatural. In the second instance, the wall has two distinct, different-colored areas which are in keeping with the observer's perception of what the wall was intended to look like.

A building with interior warm incandescent luminaires visible from the exterior may be considered aesthetically uncomfortable because of the contrast between the luminaires and the daylighted exterior. On the other hand, different-colored light sources can sometimes be used to differentiate between two distinctly different areas. For instance, hallways may be lighted with reddish incandescent to distinguish circulation paths from office spaces lighted with bluish fluorescent. Another instance in which building purpose has been clearly delineated is in a large shopping center where warm-colored lamps are predominantly used for color enrichment of merchandise, and daylight (bluish by comparison) is used to illuminate the exit areas. The emphasis on exit areas, in contrast to interior circulation areas, helps shoppers find their way out. The point to be made is that the designer of any building should be aware of the potential incompatibilities of color between electric light and daylight systems.

Another factor to be considered is the directional aspect of light. Daylight will, of course, generally enter the building through windows located in the fenestration wall, through skylights, or through clerestories. The daylight entering through skylights is easily compatible with ceiling-mounted electric fixtures because of similarities of location and light direction, but generally it will sharply contrast with indirect or task/ambient lighting systems. Seen from below, skylights which employ a diffusing material either at the roof surface or at the ceiling will produce a source of brightness similar to that of an electric fixture. People tend to find little biological satisfaction with this type of skylight installation since it provides minimal information about the exterior and produces an effect similar to the usual inert electric fixture.

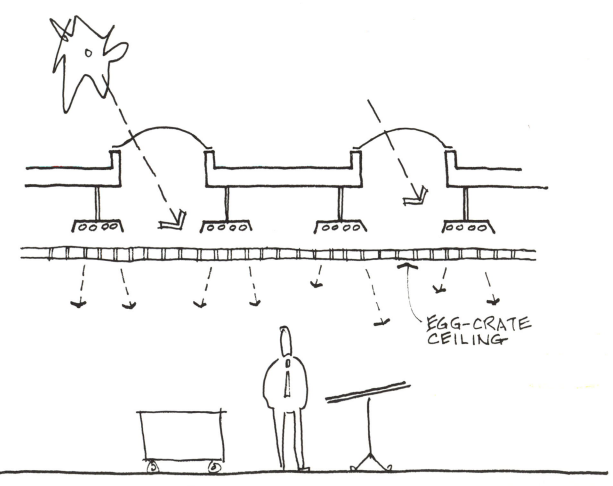

FIGURE 3-4. SKYLIGHTS CAN BE INTEGRATED WITH ELECTRIC LIGHTING.

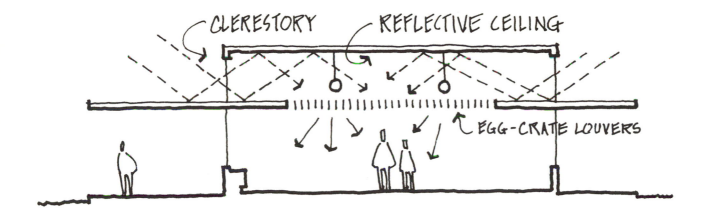

FIGURE 3-5. INTEGRATED ELECTRIC LIGHT AND DAYLIGHT IN THIS WELCOME, TEXAS, SCHOOL BY CRS ARCHITECTS.

Skylights with clear glazing, located above the ceiling line and invisible to the space occupants performing normal visual tasks, will provide greater quantities of better quality light and also satisfy needs for environmental information. Naturally, the entrance of direct sunshine through a skylight must be handled with care, and skylights should be used in appropriate areas to avoid producing excessively bright spots of sunlight around visual task areas. Skylights and clerestories are particularly more likely to be compatible with electric systems when they are used in the indirect mode (i.e., not directly visible) and mixed with the electric light. An excellent example of a well-lighted building using this principal is the Welcome, Texas, school designed by CRS in the early 1950s. As shown in Figure 2–5, both the electric lights and the clerestories are situated above the louvered ceiling so that the two sources of light mix as they enter the classroom space below. The reddish output of the incandescents, mixed with the daylight, is not noticeable.

Daylight from windows tends to flow into the interior in a generally horizontal direction even though it bounces off room surfaces, especially the ceiling, and thus takes many directions. The accent of this light from the windows highlights surfaces and objects in quite a different manner than a directly overhead bright light source. Note the difference in appearance of the objects in Figures 6a, b, and c, with the two light sources from different directions. An indirect electric light system more nearly complements the daylight, as indicated in the third frame of Figure 6c. The whole structure of the interior must allow for and complement this horizontal flow of daylight from windows for best effect.

But the electric lighting system does not always have to give way to daylight. The most appropriate lighting scheme may, because of particular programmatic characteristics, focus on the electric light system, so that the daylighting scheme is secondary and must be designed compatibly with the electric system.

FIGURE 3-6a.  Light from directly overhead.

FIGURE 3-6b.  Light from the side.

FIGURE 3-6c.  Light from the side with overhead light also.

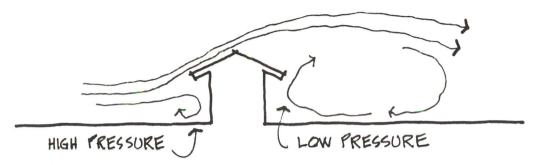

HIGH PRESSURE          LOW PRESSURE

FIGURE 3-7. AS MOVING AIR STRIKES AN OBJECT, A **HIGH-PRESSURE** AREA DEVELOPS IN FRONT, AND A **LOW-PRESSURE** AREA DOWNWIND. AIR MOVES FROM HIGH TO LOW PRESSURE.

## NATURAL AIR FLOW AND ACOUSTICS

As designers seek ways to save energy and begin to examine the concept of the window, they will naturally consider using the windows to let in some of that fresh, cool, outside air. In many parts of the country, the climate is such that the outside air can be used effectively for cooling for major portions of the year, and the windows used to admit daylight are the most logical inlets and outlets for air. Thus, the window must be considered not only for daylight, but also for its effects on other aspects of the building environment. But what happens when the windows are opened? Does all that cool air come inside to the overheated occupants? It might or it might not. Let's consider some of the things which govern the air's movement.

### Air Movement

First, air is moved by pressure differences.[2] In buildings, these pressure differences are created as the incoming air moves around and past the building. Generally, as the air strikes the building, it builds up increased pressure on the windward side, and as it separates from the building, usually at the sharp corners, it creates low-pressure areas on the downwind surfaces, as indicated in Figure 3-7. If windows on both the upwind and downwind sides of the building are opened, the air will move through, provided, of course, that its path is not blocked by internal obstructions, such as sealed-up walls. In other words, if the air can get into the building, there must be a way for it to get out. If you anticipate using the windows for fresh-air intake to cool occupants in warm weather, you must have "through ventilation." People are "air cooled" through skin moisture evaporation as the air moves across the body. Thermal currents (e.g., warm air rising from the floor to the ceiling or up a glass window heated by the sun) are not at all effective in producing sufficient air movement to cool people via this evaporation process.[3] Even the slightest breeze from the window will offset thermal gradient air movement.

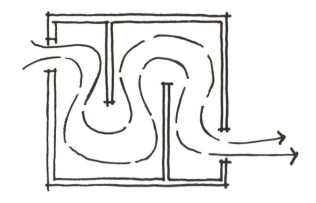

FIGURE 3-8.
CROSS VENTILATION REQUIRES A WAY FOR THE AIR TO GET OUT AS WELL AS TO GET IN.

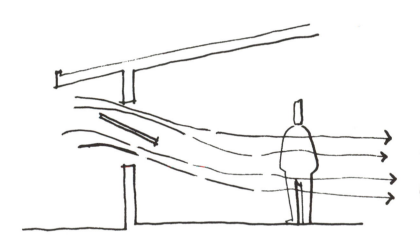

FIGURE 3-9.
AIR MOVEMENT MUST BE THROUGH THE COMFORT ZONE IF IT IS TO COOL PEOPLE.

**Windows.** The proper selection of window types, however, is necessary if the incoming air is to be usefully directed through those areas—the living zones—where occupants will be sitting or standing. Windows act as vanes directing the incoming air up, down, or to the side.[4] Air has inertia. The air will continue to move in its established direction, regardless of where the outlets are, until some additional obstruction forces it into a new direction. Figure 3-10 shows how some types of windows affect the incoming air. In the case of a vertical or horizontal sliding window that has no "vane," the incoming direction is determined by the location of the window in the fenestration, relative to the conditions of the total exterior wall and whatever obstructions may be present.[5] Figure 3-10 indicates some of these properties.

**Air Speed.** The speed with which the air moves through the building is determined by the relative sizes of the inlet and outlet. The larger the outlet in relation to the inlet, the faster the air will move. Of course, the faster the air moves, the more its cooling power will be felt. (At some point, of course, this speed may become objectionable because of blowing papers, drafts, etc.) Fig-

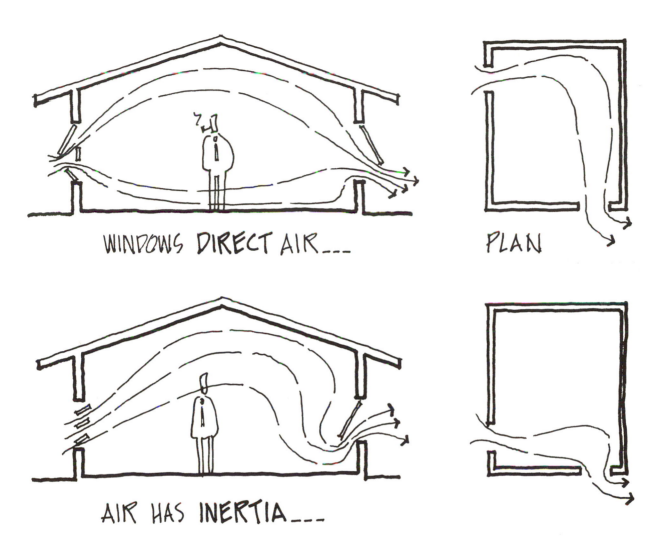

WINDOWS DIRECT AIR....

PLAN

AIR HAS INERTIA....

FIGURE 3-10. WINDOWS DIRECT INCOMING AIR MUCH AS A HOSE SQUIRTS WATER. AIR HAS INERTIA AND DOES NOT GO DIRECTLY FROM INLET TO OUTLET. WITH A SIMPLE WINDOW, ITS LOCATION IN THE WALL DETERMINES THE DIRECTION THE AIR WILL TAKE.

ure 3-11 provides air-flow speed measurements with different-sized outlets which indicate this principal.

**Clerestories and Skylights.** Clerestories, and sometimes skylights, can also be effectively used for producing air flow on the inside. Their most appropriate role is to serve as outlets since their proximity to the "living zone" makes it difficult to get the incoming air down to the living zone to provide cooling. In addition, the roof area of buildings in the majority of situations will be in a low-pressure zone (relative to the higher-pressure zone on the upwind side of the building) so that the air is naturally

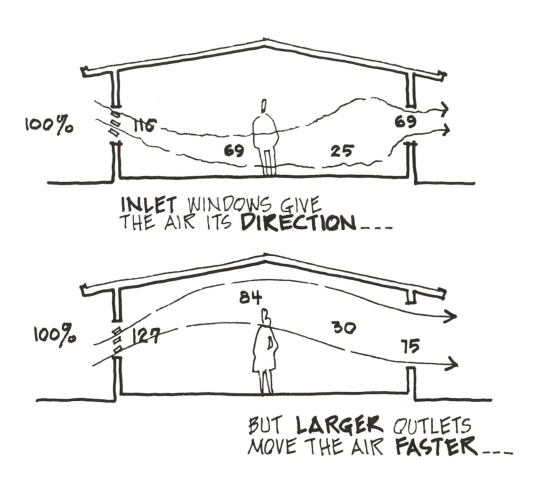

INLET WINDOWS GIVE
THE AIR ITS DIRECTION---

BUT LARGER OUTLETS
MOVE THE AIR FASTER---

FIGURE 3-11. AIR SPEED IS DETERMINED BY THE **RATIO** OF OUTLET TO INLET. THE FIGURES ON THE CROSS SECTION INDICATE **PERCENTAGE** OF OUTDOOR AIR SPEED (100 PERCENT).

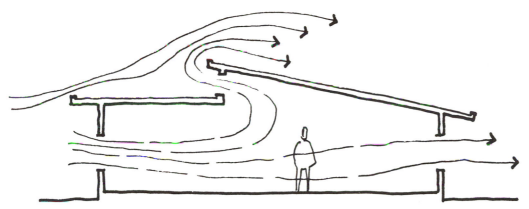

CLERESTORIES AND SKYLIGHTS MAY BE **OUTLETS**___

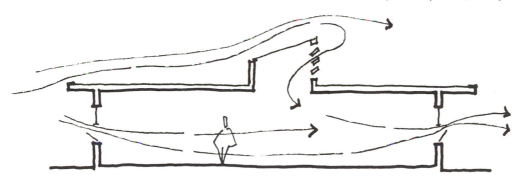

OR THEY MAY BE **INLETS**___

FIGURE 3-12. INLETS AND OUTLETS ARE DETERMINED BY WHERE THE **PRESSURE** AREAS DEVELOP.

more likely to flow out than in, through these skylights and clerestories. Figure 3-12 suggests how clerestories and skylights might be used for natural ventilation.

**Night Cooling.** Nighttime cooling of buildings during the warm weather season by bringing in the outside cool air is also becoming an important consideration in energy conservation. If windows or other openings can be opened at night, the in-coming cooler night air will help to reduce the heat stored inside the building in walls, floors, furniture, and other objects, and provide cooler conditions during the following warm day. In many areas of the country, the application of this technique during the warm season would provide sufficiently comfortable conditions so that the air conditioning, otherwise considered necessary, would not be needed or, at least, might be reduced.

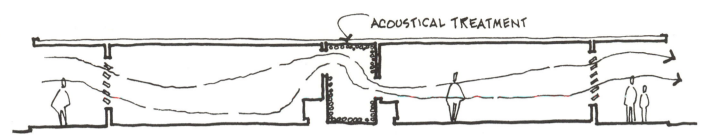

FIGURE 3-13. THIS ELEMENTARY SCHOOL BY ARCHITECTS CRS UTILIZES CROSS VENTILATION AND AN ACOUSTICALLY TREATED UTILITY CORE.

The process of designing a building, locating openings in the building, or orienting the building to the site so as to create this cross-ventilation air movement is a tricky business. The understanding of some of the basic principles of air movement is absolutely necessary. But definitive answers to air-flow problems can be realized only through studies of building models, preferably tested in a wind tunnel.

## Acoustics

Providing openings in otherwise sealed-up buildings also introduces potential acoustic problems. Noise from exterior activities such as streets and playgrounds can be a significant nuisance and, if excessive, the use of natural air movement for cooling may not be feasible.

Acoustic problems may also occur if openings in interior partitions are provided to allow air to pass from one space or room to another. The transfer of interior noise can be reduced considerably through proper use of materials with high acoustic absorption and by the off-setting of partition openings so that the path of the sound is not direct from source to receiver.

In the design of a low-budget elementary school for Laredo, Texas, before the period when air conditioning of schools was common, architects CRS developed a design with a central plenum chamber between classrooms to allow air to pass between the rooms and to be used as an area for placing acoustical absorptive materials. The sketch in Figure 3-13 indicates the general design scheme. The acoustic results were apparently satisfactory, and students in the downwind classroom, whose ventilation came out of the plenum chamber via a typical air-conditioning-type grill, received an additional psychological comfort boost, as if the room were in fact air conditioned.

## SOLAR ENERGY

It is one of those basic facts of life that where there is light there is also heat. In the radiant energy spectrum, the energy radiation that produces light (the visible portion), overlaps considerably with radiant energy that produces a sensation of warmth in humans (the near and far infrared wavelengths). This overlap applies to all forms of light, whether "natural" or "manufactured." For most common types of electric light, the heat contribution per lumen of light produced exceeds that of daylight. In other words, we get less heat contribution per unit of light with daylight than we do with electric light. (Recent improvements in lamps and luminaires have somewhat decreased the heat contributions from some types of electric lights, but new developments in glasses have also provided for reduced heat contribution from daylight.)

So, if buildings use windows to admit daylight, the windows will also admit a certain amount of warming radiant energy. Naturally, this helps in the winter, but it also can pose a problem during warm weather and the air-conditioning season. The problem for designers is how to get the desired daylight in, while at the same time admitting either a lot of heat or very little heat, depending on what is desired at a particular time of the year.

Unfortunately, many of the passive solar heating buildings going up these days focus on heat input at the expense of daylighting. Some designers are not aware that letting all that radiant heat into the building can create objectionable and, often, impossible seeing conditions. There is little point in going over all of the basic concepts of passive design for shading and heating buildings with the sun's energy. The subject has been profusely and thoroughly covered in many publications in recent years. However, a few points deserve emphasis.

Generally, light from the sun, or even from the sky, is many times greater than that required for good visibility in most buildings and for most tasks. The same is true for heat from the sun and sky. Given an environmental enclosure that would admit all of the light and heat impinging upon it without losing any, the space would be intolerably hot and would usually have an illumination level of several thousand footcandles. Thus, if buildings are properly designed to effectively utilize daylight, they can reject the majority of the direct light from the sun and sky, but still let in an ample supply. This simple fact provides opportunities for manipulating the sun's energy to allow or reject heat without destroying its daylight benefits. Passive solar energy enthusiasts should exercise extreme caution to avoid providing heat at the expense of visibility.

The simplest kind of overhang on the south of a building still offers one of the most effective methods for handling the sun's light and heat. In the summer, a properly designed overhang keeps the sun's direct rays off glass areas while allowing plenty of daylight to enter via reflection from the ground. In the winter, the overhang allows the low-angle sun to penetrate for warmth, but care must be exercised to avoid visibility problems. The overhang reduces somewhat the area of bright sky visible from within the building (which is good) and reflects light from the ground, low in heat content, deep into the room for better light distribution. Vertical baffles effectively control sun and light on east and west building facades when the sun is low in the sky.

Clear glass allows 75 to 80 percent of the sun's warming infrared waves to penetrate into the building. Shading devices used on the inside of the building can reflect some of that radiant energy back to the exterior so that the energy heating the space is 30 to 40 percent of the total radiant energy from the sun striking the glass. Exterior shading devices can reduce that radiant energy penetration to 5 to 10 percent. Because the atmosphere absorbs and reflects a higher percent of infrared waves than visible waves, the light from the sky produces less radiant energy on the ground per unit of light than does light directly from the sun. Exterior shading devices have not been used as frequently in the last 20 years as in previous decades because of the cost of construction and maintenance. Their costs, however, should be compared to alternative designs on a life cycle cost basis for a best solution.

## VIEW

Although daylight and view are often thought to be inseparable, they do not necessarily go together and, in fact, very often should not be achieved through the same aperture. The criteria for producing a view to the exterior are not the same as for producing good interior daylight. Daylight can be bounced into a space for over-all distri-

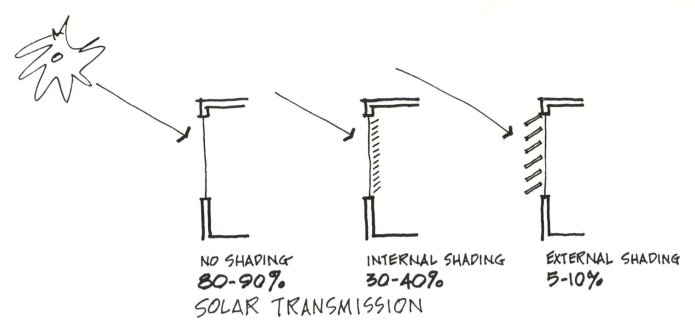

NO SHADING
80-90%

INTERNAL SHADING
30-40%

EXTERNAL SHADING
5-10%

SOLAR TRANSMISSION

FIGURE 3-14. EXTERIOR SHADING DEVICES CAN **REDUCE** THE SUN'S **HEAT** CONTRIBUTION BY AS MUCH AS 90 TO 95 PERCENT.

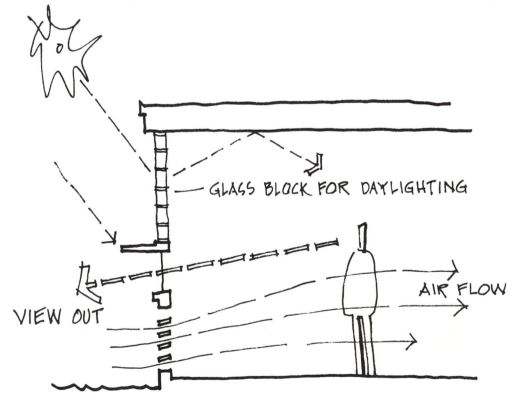

GLASS BLOCK FOR DAYLIGHTING

VIEW OUT

AIR FLOW

FIGURE 3-15. DAYLIGHT AND VIEW DO NOT ALWAYS GO TOGETHER.

bution and brightness control, but the view out must be direct. An excessively bright outdoors can be made more palatable to the view with tinted glazing, but the tinted material reduces the daylight contribution to the indoors. However, since daylight and view so often are found together in the form of a window, a few remarks about view are in order.

It is certain that some people who express a strong preference for the presence of daylight in a space may actually be as much concerned about the ability to see out as they are about daylight. And while the presence of daylight helps to satisfy some biological needs with regard to the changing nature of the weather, certain other needs are directly associated with a view—activity participation, relaxation, and the need for information about the environment. The view especially satisfies the desire for a sense of participation in the activities of the "real" world outside. People who work or live in view-restricted spaces may develop symptoms of claustrophobia and, consciously or unconsciously, expend energy and perhaps time in idleness because of the lack of information about the world around them. It is not uncommon to see employees in such surroundings leave their work to seek some type of contact with the outdoors.

A view to the outdoors is also very helpful in reducing the fatigue that accompanies highly concentrated visual attention to a task. The ability to direct eye attention away from the immediate indoor task and focus on distant objects is relaxing to the eyes and, hence, to the mind. A good view is often the right medicine.

Almost any view is better than no view, but a good view out is one which provides the right type of information content. Information, for instance, about the weather is one of the most important aspects of a view. Another is the season of the year, indicated by the condition of the vegetation. Another is the activity of persons on the outside, although at times this can be distracting. This view, in terms of information content, may be divided into three areas: the sky (upward), the landscape (horizontal), and the ground (downward). The best views are the ones which include some

portion of all three areas.[6] The sky provides information about the weather, the horizon provides the information which helps maintain a sense of orientation and balance, and the ground provides information about more specific community activities.

An architectural student lives in a house close to a beautiful mountain with some very nice windows which look toward the mountain. He complains, however, that the view is "lousy," since he is so close to the mountain that all he can see from the windows is the ground and the vegetation which grows on the side of the mountain— no sky and no horizon. The information content of the view from his windows is minimal.

People also like to see changes as they view the exterior. They prefer a more complex structural organization of information content with a wide range of variations. A view of static conditions, no matter how beautiful, may become monotonous very quickly.

The presence of a view from a building is in many ways a very subjective asset, and clients often seek more concrete evidence that windows, view, and daylight are, in fact, economically justifiable. While not all things of value (such as a view of beautiful Pike's Peak) are easily proven cost-effective, there are methods by which value can be established. For instance, if a space with a window in an office building commands a higher rental income than a windowless space, the view then does have financial value, even if the higher rent is based on user preference alone.

## SUMMARY

Successful architecture requires the simultaneous integration of a variety of environmental concerns, including climatic, biological, psychological, and perceptive effects. The architect must somehow find a single, buildable design scheme that will best respond to all these concerns. Failure to find a scheme which appropriately responds to any *one* of them may well result in disaster for the total scheme. An understanding of human responsiveness on all fronts is necessary before consideration can be given to the specific interrelationships of daylighting and architecture.

# HOW DAYLIGHT BEHAVES IN ARCHITECTURE

The study of how light behaves in buildings can be most meaningful if it relates to specific goals. So often, designers indicate various glass openings in a building design for which there is no apparent reason beyond creating a "delightful" environment. Transparent openings or panels are useful for a variety of purposes, but a good look at some recently designed "daylighted" buildings may well lead to the question, "What did the designer intend to accomplish with daylight?" This question when put to the designer may well indicate that his goals were not very specific or well defined, even if the results turned out to be exciting. Architects are notorious for designing from the "seat of their pants"—sometimes the results are exciting and sometimes disappointing. But there are specific, tangible design goals which made good sense in almost all cases and which can guide the designer in creating a meaningful and delightful building.

Let us hasten to add, however, that creative design often intuitively produces results which inspire the human soul and for which there is little in the way of conventional rationale. The great designers in history often achieved magnificent results without following conventional logic. Most of us will stay out of trouble if we combine creativity and sensitivity with a firm grasp of fundamentals.

## GOALS FOR GOOD DAYLIGHTING

First, we need to get as much daylight as possible as deep as possible into the building interior. Within the normal parameters of interior lighting, there is no such thing as too much light. The human eye can adjust to intensity levels producing several thousands of footlamberts of luminance without discomfort and, generally, the more light there is, the better people can see. (Excessive brightness differences and veiling reflections are separate issues.) And the more light there is deep in the interior, the less electric light will be needed and the less energy consumed.

Second, we need to control in some way the brightnesses of surfaces within the field of view, both within and without the building, to avoid those excessive brightness differences that reduce visibility.

Third, we need to avoid creating conditions within the building that may allow disabling veiling reflections to occur where there may be critical tasks, or we need, at least, to limit the opportunity for veiling reflections to the minimum amount of floor area possible.

But let's not forget that all tasks are not of a critical nature. In our normal activities we address ourselves to a variety of visual tasks in the environment which are critical to different degrees and which require different levels of visibility. Writing the day's grocery list at the kitchen table does not require the same visibility nor have the same significance in case of error as inspecting ball bearings on an assembly line. There are many tasks in the environment to be lighted which will require a high degree of visibility. People can see and enjoy red-carpeted floors, tiled walls, spiral staircases, antique furniture, cut flowers, and other people, for instance, without large quantities of glare-free lighting.

Thus, we need two types of lighting: *task lighting,* for a variety of tasks as well as for critical tasks, and *ambient lighting,* for general movement, observation, and orientation.

## GUIDELINES FOR GOOD DAYLIGHTING

### Avoid Direct Skylight and Sunshine on Critical Tasks

The easiest way to get plenty of daylight into a space is to use very large openings—clear glass windows, clerestories, or skylights—with a minimum of controls. But direct sunshine in the vicinity of critical task areas and a direct view of the sky from these areas will expose occupants to excessive brightness differences that will result in poor visibility and discomfort.

### Use Direct Skylight and Sunshine Sparingly in Non-critical Task Areas

Direct sunshine can add excitement to architecture. It provides opportunity for changing patterns of light and shadow on interior surfaces and objects. It can give occupants a sense of well-being, of time, and orientation, but it must be used with discretion or it is likely to cause poor seeing conditions or add excessive heat to a space.

### Bounce Daylight Off Surrounding Surfaces

The daylight that reaches our tasks, while originating with the sun, in effect, comes from nearly all surfaces and objects around us by way of reflections. Each time the daylight is reflected from a surface, it is spread and softened. Light that is spread over large areas and reflected is partially absorbed and, thus, reduced in intensity, but the process spreads and evens the general brightness patterns, increasing visibility and seeing comfort.

### Bring the Daylight in High

The higher the light opening is, the deeper daylight will penetrate into the interior space, and the less likely the opening will allow excessive exterior brightnesses into the field of view. The light that comes in high is more likely to be softened and spread by surfaces and objects before it gets to task level.

### Filter the Daylight

The harshness of direct skylight and direct sun can be filtered for additional softness

# FIGURE 4-1. AVOID DIRECT
## SUNLIGHT AND SKYLIGHT _____

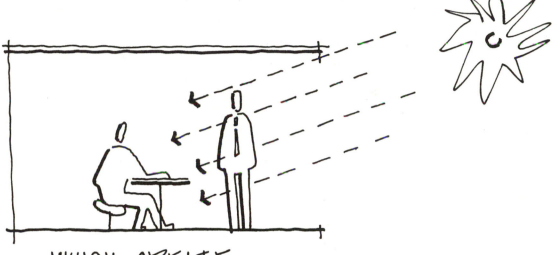

_ _ _ WHICH CREATE
EXCESSIVE BRIGHTNESS DIFFERENCES

# FIGURE 4-2. USE DIRECT SUNSHINE
## SPARINGLY IN NON-CRITICAL TASK AREAS _ _ _

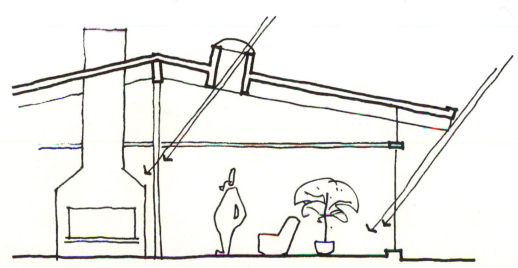

# FIGURE 4-3. BOUNCE DAYLIGHT OFF SURROUNDING SURFACES___

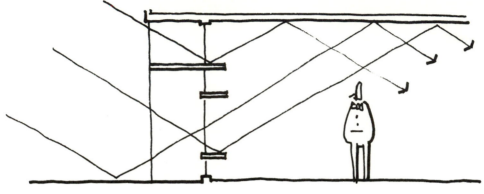

TO SOFTEN AND SPREAD IT

# FIGURE 4-4. BRING DAYLIGHT IN HIGH___

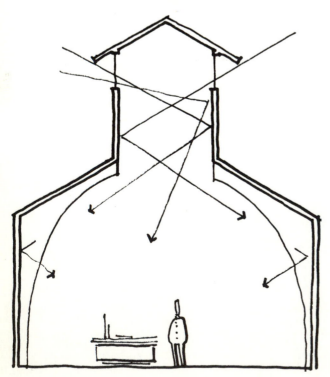

___ AND LET IT DOWN SOFTLY

# FIGURE 4-5. FILTER THE DAYLIGHT___

## WITH TREES AND PLANTS___     DRAPES OR SCREENS

and more uniform distribution. Even electric luminaires are not left exposed, naked to the eye. They are surrounded with devices to filter or reflect the light so that its intensity is spread and softened. Trees, shrubs, vines, curtains, reflective "shelves," and louvers are effective tools for filtering daylight as it enters building spaces.

**Integrate Daylight with Other Environmental Concerns**
Design for daylight should be modified by, and integrated with, other environmental concerns. View, natural air movement, acoustics, and electric lighting are all elements which must be considered when designing openings for daylight. A change in

# FIGURE 4-6. INTEGRATE DAYLIGHT
## WITH OTHER ENVIRONMENTAL CONCERNS___

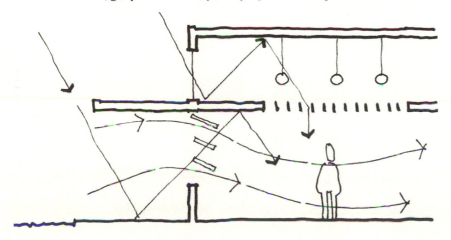

building or component design in response to one element of the environment is likely to affect the response to other elements—an operable window to allow daylight and natural air flow will also allow noise to enter the space. All environmental factors must be considered simultaneously.

## FORM-GIVING FACTORS

There are a number of light-controlling design considerations which may significantly affect the shape and form of a building. Probably the most significant design determinant in the use of daylight is the geometry of the building—the walls, ceilings, floors, windows, and how they relate to each other. Some of our most significant buildings have been shaped by considerations for daylight—the early Greek and Egyptian temples, the Gothic cathedrals of the 13th and 14th centuries, school buildings of the early 20th century, and some of our most admired recent buildings by Kahn, Wright, Aalto, and Caudill. An understanding of the effects of various building elements on daylighting provides the basis for manipulating form to achieve adequate lighting levels. Remember that the material presented in these accompanying illustrations has mostly to do with distribution of intensity due to the building form, and little to do with luminance or brightness quality.

While it is important to understand geometric relationships in terms of lighting function, it is also valuable to begin to grasp the quantitative relationships that go with various geometric forms. Designers often ask, "I understand how the walls reflect light, but *how much* light will I get?" A review of measured illumination levels for various types of building designs will be somewhat helpful, but experience is also a good teacher. Designers should manipulate the forms and measure the results before they can really understand the quantitative relationships. Such experience can be easily acquired through model studies, which are discussed in Chapter 7. The data that follows is taken from work performed at the Texas Engineering Experiment Station in 1950–51.[1] It will help in the understanding of the basic relationships of form and material.

### Window Height

The window size and height above the workplace are among the most important factors in daylighting design. Naturally, as the window becomes larger in size, the amount of daylight admitted increases. But the *height* of the windows is the more significant factor. The higher the window, the deeper the daylight will penetrate into the room. The test data shown in Figures 4–7a and 4–7b indicate the effects of changes in window height on a non-dimensional graph superimposed on a cross section of a rectangular room 28 feet deep. (These and subsequent tests were conducted under an overcast sky.) When the ceiling was lowered from 14 to 12 feet, the illumination at a point near the back (windowless) wall decreased about 19 percent. About the same percentage in illumination loss occurred when the window head was lowered from 12 to 10 feet, and also from 10 to 8 feet. Remember that these figures are true only for these particular conditions. The tests were made with surface reflectances of 85 percent for the ceiling, 60 percent for the walls, and 40 percent for the floor.

Notice also that the distribution of light in the room changed. In the case of the 14-foot ceiling, there was a drop in illumination from near the window side to near the rear wall of 2.6:1.0, while the ratio of distribution in the room with the 8-foot ceiling was on the order of 4:1. Thus, high windows provide a more even distribution of illumination as well as an increase in general quantity. In a similar room with windows on two sides, the intensity decreases and the diversity of illumination decreases with a decrease in window height, but not to such a great extent as in the unilaterally lighted room.

### Room Depth

How deep into a room will daylight penetrate? It depends on how high the ceiling is (or how high the top of the window is), but let's look at the effects of room depth on task-level illumination if the ceiling and window head height are held constant. Figure 4–10 shows the results of tests on a room with a 12-foot ceiling using room depths of 24 feet, 28 feet, and 32 feet. The results

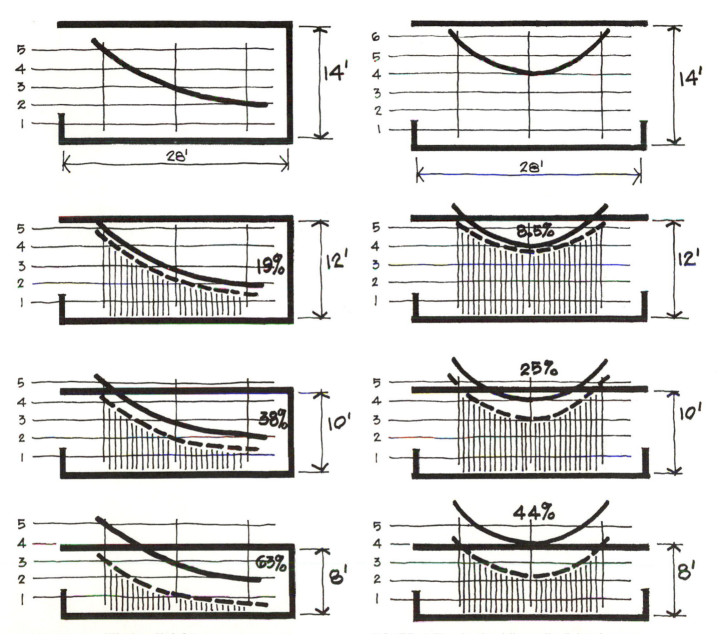

FIGURE 4-7a. **Window Height:** As the height of the window is reduced from 14 feet to 12 feet, there is a 19 percent drop in illumination in the back of the unilaterally lighted room, as indicated on the graph superimposed on a cross section.

FIGURE 4-7b. In the bilaterally lighted room, there is an 8.5 percent drop at the center of the room. Further lowering of the window height results in reduced illumination levels, but the reductions are not so pronounced as in the unilateral room.

FIGURES 4-8 & 4-9.   These very high windows in this Kansas City shopping area bring daylight deep into the interior and distribute it evenly.

show that as the room was made deeper, the level of intensity throughout became less—a simple matter of spreading the same quantity of incoming light over a larger area. The 28-foot-deep room had 18 percent less light at a point near the back wall than at the same relative position in the 24-foot room. There was a 28 percent drop in the case of the 32-foot room.

Note also that the distribution of light across the room became more diverse as the room got deeper. In the 24-foot room, the ratio of maximum to minimum intensity was 2.6:1.0; in the 32-foot room, it was 3.0:1.0.

Some states have had, and may still have, codes which specify minimum ceiling heights in certain types of buildings, schools for instance, without suggesting any limitation on room depth. Such codes are patently ridiculous. A particular window head or ceiling height may be quite satisfactory with a room depth of 18 feet, but would be very poor for a room depth of 40 feet. The room proportions are more important than any specific dimension.

The old rule of thumb (in some cases, code regulation) that says that the depth of the room should not be more than two and one-half times the height of the window wall is not a bad one—for unilaterally lighted rooms. However, considering the possibilities of daylighting rooms with window openings in more than one wall and with the use of skylights—all contributing to increased intensity levels and better light distribution—the idea of trying to stipulate good daylighting with some prescriptive regulation is self-defeating.

## Window Width

The results of tests (Figure 4–11) on spaces with 24-foot depths, 12-foot ceilings, and lengths of 36 feet, 28 feet, and 20 feet show that in a unilaterally lighted space, wide windows provide higher levels of illumination than do narrow windows—not much, but there is a difference. The tests showed that when a 36-foot-wide window wall was shortened to 28 feet, there was a 7 percent drop in intensity at a point near the back wall. When the 36-foot window was reduced to 20 feet, there was a reduction of 25 percent.

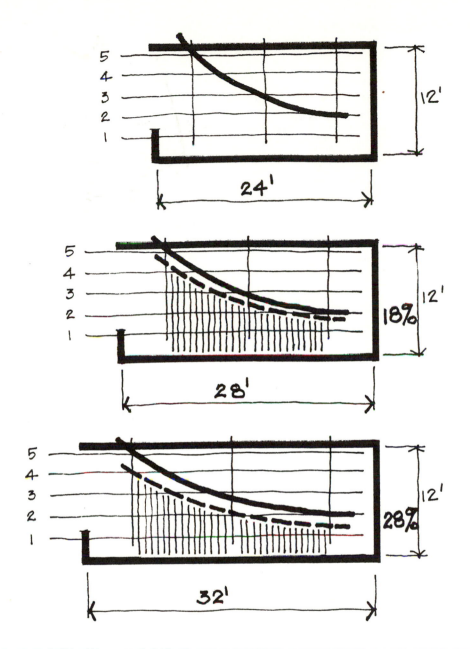

FIGURE 4-10. ROOM DEPTH: THE RESULT
OF THE ROOMS WITH DIFFERENT DEPTHS
SHOWS REDUCED DAYLIGHT LEVELS ON THE
GRAPH SUPERIMPOSED ON A CROSS SECTION.
THERE WAS A 28 PERCENT REDUCTION IN
ILLUMINATION AT A POINT IN BACK OF THE ROOM
AS THE DEPTH WAS INCREASED FROM 24 FEET
TO 32 FEET.

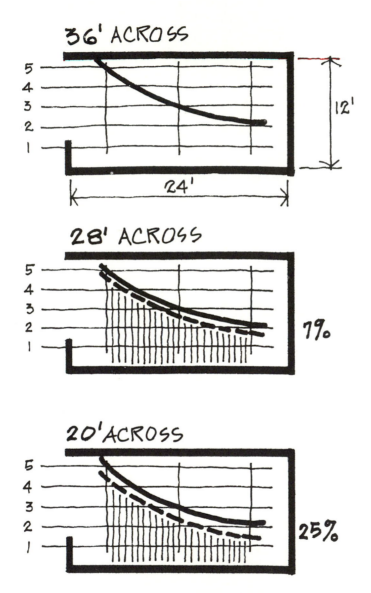

FIGURE 4-11. WINDOW WIDTH: WHEN THE WIDTH OF THE WINDOWS (AND ROOM) IS REDUCED, THE ILLUMINATION IN THE BACK OF THE ROOM IS ALSO REDUCED.

## Sloping Ceilings

Sloping ceilings are often thought of as a viable technique for reflecting light into a space and thereby increasing the level of illumination. Tests on a 24-foot-deep, unilaterally lighted room with a 12-foot-high ceiling—first with a flat ceiling and then with a ceiling sloped to a height of 7 feet—indicate no measurable difference in intensity levels at desk height.

## Overhangs

Building overhangs can be very useful for sun control and rain control and, although they do reduce the level of light intensity within the building, particularly next to the window wall, they are especially effective in collecting light reflected from the ground and further reflecting it back into the interior of the building. The result is a more even distribution of light in the space.

The test results shown in Figure 4–13 indicate a 39 percent drop in illumination near the window of a unilaterally lighted room with the addition of a 6-foot overhang, but only a 22 percent drop near the interior wall. In a similar room with windows in opposite walls, the addition of 6-foot overhangs over both windows reduced the illumination near the windows by 34 percent and at the center of the room by 25 percent.

Overhangs are also helpful in reducing the area of sky that can be seen from within the room, although the effect is minimal.

## Skylights

Skylights are excellent devices for picking up large quantities of light with minimum-

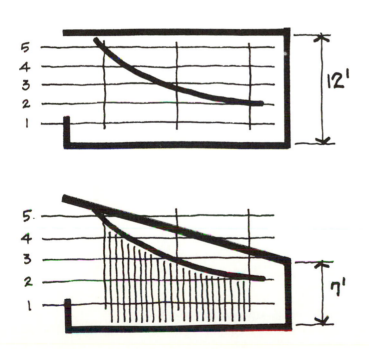

FIGURE 4-12. SLOPING CEILINGS: SLOPING CEILINGS HAVE NO SIGNIFICANT EFFECT ON DAYLIGHT ON THE TASK.

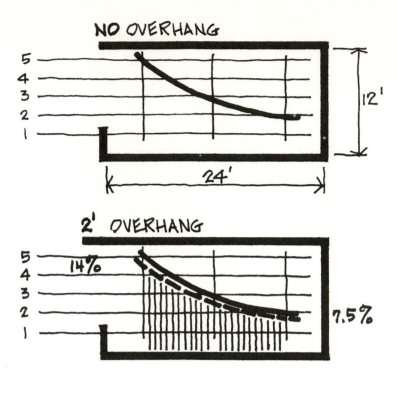

**NO OVERHANG**

**2' OVERHANG**

14%

7.5%

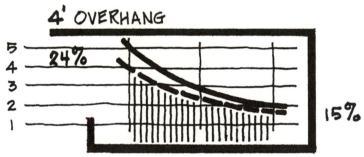

**4' OVERHANG**

24%

15%

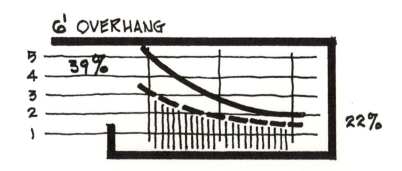

**6' OVERHANG**

39%

22%

## OVERHANGS-UNILATERAL

FIGURES 4-13. OVERHANGS: A SIX-FOOT OVERHANG PRODUCES LESS OF A **REDUCTION**

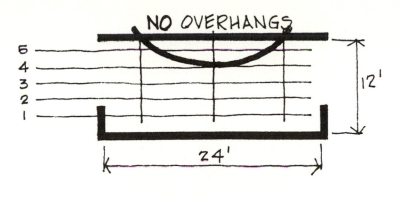

NO OVERHANGS

5 4 3 2 1

12'

24'

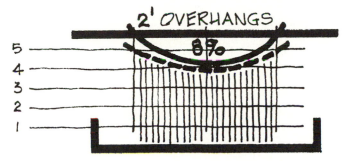

2' OVERHANGS

8%

5 4 3 2 1

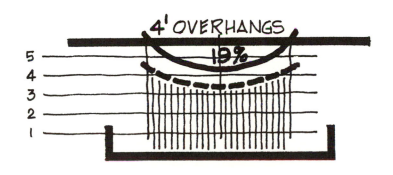

4' OVERHANGS

19%

5 4 3 2 1

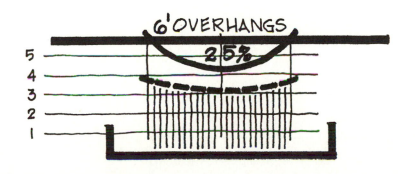

6' OVERHANGS

25%

5 4 3 2 1

# OVERHANGS - BILATERAL

OF ILLUMINATION IN THE **BACK** OF THE ROOM
THAN NEXT TO THE WINDOW WALL.

sized openings. The illumination falling on the horizontal plane of the roof may be many times that which strikes the vertical plane of the window wall even under an overcast sky.

Skylights are effective tools for delivering daylight deep into interior areas of one-story buildings or into the top floors of multistory buildings.[2] They can even be used to bring daylight into the lower floors of multistory buildings through plenums, light wells, and reflective devices, although the economics of such designs will depend on the particular conditions involved.

Skylights come in a variety of sizes and shapes—they can be custom made to almost any design. They may include glass glazing—clear, patterned, or translucent—or glazing with a variety of types of plastics. While the general principles which govern their performance apply to all types of skylights and all types of glazing, the most common variety is the plastic-dome skylight. Generally consisting of an aluminum frame and one or more vacuum-formed domes of acrylic plastic, these skylights are relatively inexpensive, easy to install, rain proof, and long lasting. Acrylic plastics may be clear, grey tinted, or diffuse (sometimes called "smoky white" or white translucent). Acrylics have excellent optical properties, similar to glass, are relatively easy to maintain, and may last up to 20 or 30 years. Some domed skylights are made

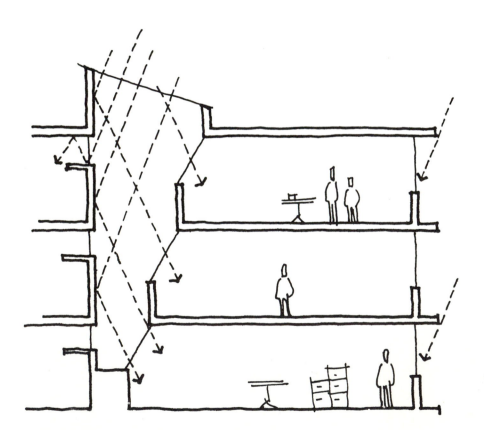

FIGURE 4-14. SKYLIGHTS CAN DELIVER DAYLIGHT DEEP INTO INTERIORS

with fiberglass-reinforced polyester, which is diffuse and cannot be made transparent. This plastic is generally less costly, but tends to deteriorate with time and must occasionally be recoated.

Some manufacturers claim that the plastic-dome skylight is "self-cleaning" with rain. In several tests of actual installations, this was found to be generally true, but it is dependent upon the amount and type of pollution in the air, the extent of early morning dew, and the amount and frequency of rain. What is more significant, perhaps, is that more dirt was deposited on the inside of the plastic domes than on the outside, particularly in environments with significant contaminants in the air. Some pro-

FIGURE 4-15. This clear glass skylight at the offices of CRS, architects, is a design feature in the entrance walkway.

FIGURE 4-16. The big clear glass skylight lights the CRS reception area below.

FIGURE 4-17. Roof skylights on a factory.

FIGURE 4-18. Warehouse.
Photo: N. Bleecker Green

gram of periodic cleaning is as important with skylights as with electric luminaires.

The largest use of plastic-dome skylights is in the roofs of warehouses and light industrial buildings, where the major objective is a minimum quantity of light for the least cost. Skylights used in these situations are almost always made of diffuse plastic, which reduces total transmission of light and heat and disperses the light in all directions. In an environment where intensity levels may be as low as a few footcandles, these diffuse skylights may cause brightness contrast problems, but since the visual requirements are usually minimal anyway, (moving boxes, stacking tires, welding, fitting pipes, etc.) difficult brightness conditions are tolerated.

In environments where visual conditions are more demanding, such as classrooms and offices, the plastic-dome, diffuse skylight, if directly exposed to view from below, is very likely to produce excessive brightness and to cause disabling veiling reflections on tasks below, just as electric luminaires can. However, daylight from skylights can be controlled through the use of deep wells, splayed wells, and louvers, eliminating any view of the dome from below and minimizing the veiling reflection problem. Diffuse plastic or glass in skylights tends to diminish the biological benefits of daylight by modifying the visual effects of the weather. There seems little logic in using diffusing materials. Clear glass or plastic which allows direct sun to penetrate the skylight works well so long as some light control element is used to prevent the direct sun from interfering with visual conditions below.

It is true that the use of the clear plastic dome may allow a greater amount of the sun's heat as well as light to penetrate. This is often used as an argument in favor of a diffuse dome which reflects a portion of the heat. But domes with clear plastic, which also allow a higher percentage of daylight penetration, need not be as large as openings with diffusing domes.

Skylights with clear glass or plastic and direct sun will produce more internal heat for a given unit of illumination at task level

FIGURE 4-19. Skylights in a residence.
Photo: Norman McGrath

inside than comparable skylights with diffuse glazing, because of the behavioral characteristics of radiant energy. A good case can be made for providing some type of exterior shield that will shade the skylight from direct sun as a means of reducing the heat load while still allowing ample daylight to penetrate from the sky alone.

Double-domes (two thicknesses of plastic with an air space between) are recommended for colder climates as a means of reducing conductive heat loss in winter.[3] Some building codes include a requirement that for climates with more than 2500 heating degree-days, double-domes must be used. The value of the double-dome is somewhat reduced in warmer climates where radiant heat gains are more significant than conductive losses.

FIGURE 4-20. This skylight is bronze tinted and provides good biological relationships with the exterior. Photo: Philip Turner

FIGURE 4-22. This tinted glass skylight in The Galleria, Houston, brings daylight into the shopping center ice arena.

FIGURE 4-21. These skylights in the Hearst Memorial Mining Building on the University of California (Berkeley) campus add grace and charm to this fine old building.

FIGURE 4-23. This combination of side-wall and skylight lighting produces a well-daylighted space in this atrium at The Galleria in Houston.

On the plus side, skylights reduce energy consumption by admitting daylight and eliminating the need for some electric light. They also admit heat from the sun in the winter, reducing the need for internal heating—which can be significant. On the negative side, skylights lose some interior heat and electric light to the cooler outside air, and they admit heat from the outside during the air-conditioning season. The determination of whether skylights are economically viable in a particular situation, must include a year-round analysis of both positive and negative aspects based on local climatic conditions. A properly designed and utilized skylight system with daylight and heat-transfer controls for both day and night conditions will prove viable on a year-round basis in almost all localities.

## Clerestories

Clerestories have most of the attributes of skylights except that they occur in the vertical rather than the horizontal plane and,

FIGURE 4-24. Buckminster Fuller's geodesic dome for Expo '67 in Montreal used clear glazing to produce "exterior" lighting. (Who worried about energy use in those days?)

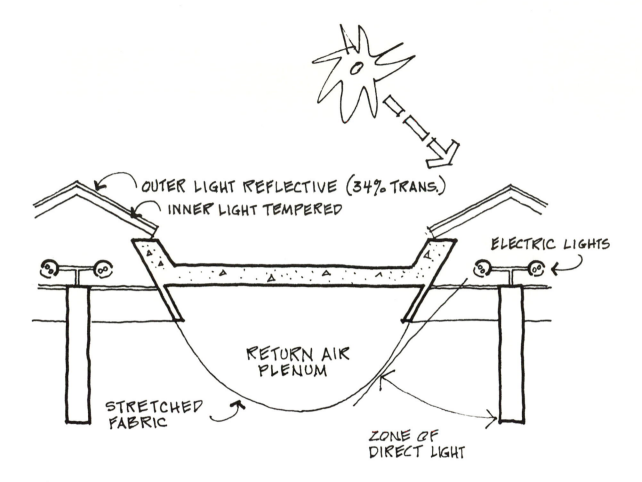

OUTER LIGHT REFLECTIVE (34% TRANS.)

INNER LIGHT TEMPERED

ELECTRIC LIGHTS

RETURN AIR PLENUM

STRETCHED FABRIC

ZONE OF DIRECT LIGHT

FIGURE 4-25.  JOHN CARL WARNECKE & ASSOCIATES AVOIDED DIRECT VIEW OF SKYLIGHTS THROUGH THIS UNIQUE SHIELDING SYSTEM IN THE AID FOR LUTHERANS BUILDING.

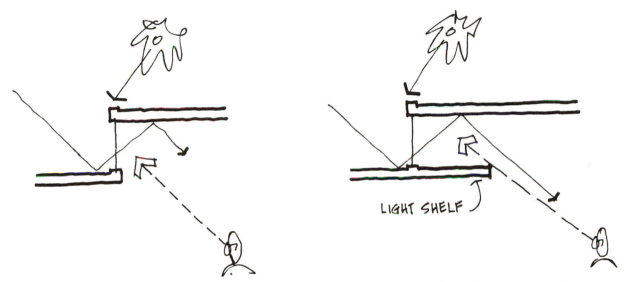

CLERESTORIES MAY ALLOW **DIRECT** VIEW OF SKY___ OR THEY MAY NOT.
THEY MAY BE ORIENTED **AWAY** FROM THE SUN, OR___
**INTO THE SUN.**

FIGURE 4-26. CLERESTORIES CAN BOUNCE GREAT
QUANTITIES OF DAYLIGHT AND CAN CONTROL DIRECT
SUN AND **VISION** TO THE EXTERIOR.

FIGURE 4-27.  Harvard's Gund Hall uses clerestories over the studio areas for ambient and task lighting.

FIGURE 4-28.  These clerestories at Boston's Logan International Airport eliminate the need for electric lights much of the year.

therefore, are exposed to less quantities of daylight than are skylights and can be oriented to prevent penetration of direct sun. When built in combination with a lightshelf, a clerestory can bounce great quantities of daylight against the upper ceiling, providing significant quantities of illumination on the tasks below and, at the same time, blocking the view of the bright sky from below. The penetration of direct sun through clerestories can be eliminated with proper orientation or with the addition of overhangs and horizontal louvers on the interior or exterior.

George Gund Hall on the Harvard campus (Figure 4-27), designed by John Andrews, Architects, demonstrates several characteristics of stepped clerestories. Note that where the partly cloudy sky is shielded from view from the interior by trees and buildings on the outside, the effect is quite pleasant. When the sky can be seen directly through the clear glass, the contrast between the interior and exterior tends to be uncomfortable. Note the fiberglass-reinforced polyester used to cover the upper chord of the roof truss. This translucent material creates excessive brightness in contrast to the interior surfaces and the view through the clear glass. The general level of illumination in Gund Hall is surprisingly comfortable.

## Recessed Windows and Splayed Jambs

Windows and other daylight apertures which are set essentially flush in a wall or ceiling, tend to produce excessive contrasts between exterior brightnesses and the interior surfaces immediately adjacent to the aperture. Perception of the sharp contrast between the exterior and interior areas is harsh and uncomfortable. A "softer" transition between the two can be achieved through the use of splayed jambs, as indicated in Figure 29. Instead of the sharp contrast between perpendicular surfaces, the splayed jamb provides a zone of intermediate brightness which "softens" the change. Thomas Jefferson used the concept effectively in his design of the Rotunda at the University of Virginia. A similar effect can result from rounded jambs or from walls which are slanted toward the window opening.

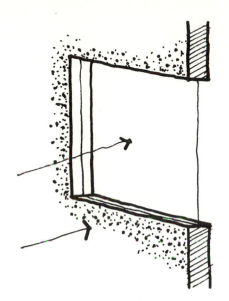

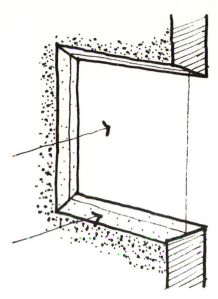

**FLUSH** OPENINGS PRODUCE SHARP **CONTRASTS**

**SPLAYED** WINDOW JAMBS **SOFTEN** CONTRASTS

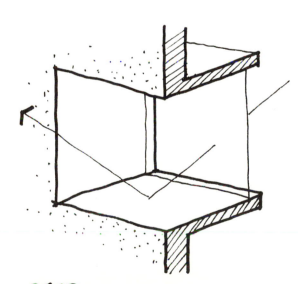

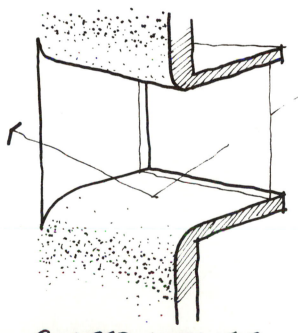

**DEEP** WINDOW WELLS HELP **SOFTEN** DAYLIGHT AND CONTRASTS

**ROUNDED** JAMBS HELP **SOFTEN** CONTRASTS

FIGURE 4-29. RECESSED WINDOWS AND SPLAYED JAMBS CAN BE EFFECTIVE ELEMENTS IN SOFTENING BRIGHTNESS CONTRASTS.

FIGURE 4-30. Splayed window jambs in the Rotunda at the University of Virginia, designed by Thomas Jefferson, produce a delightfully soft interior.

Daylight apertures which have recessed jambs or which are set deep in the wall, will also present less of a brightness contrast problem than flush openings. Since we frequently view windows from an angle rather than straight on, a deeply recessed window will allow less of a view of exterior brightnesses and provide more of a soft transition. The jambs of the window here become light-reflecting shelves to bounce the light indirectly into the interior space. Medieval buildings, with their tendency toward heavy, thick walls, provide some beautiful examples of this principle. Exterior overhangs and louvers and interior shades and louvers can be used for desired sun and light control.

## Surface Reflectances

To understand the effects of various wall surfaces in a typical type of rectangular room, let's make some comparisons. In the room shown in Figure 4-31, all the room surfaces have been painted white, and the minimum illumination in the room at point "x," whatever the footcandle level is, is assumed to be 100 percent. If the back wall (away from the window wall) is painted a flat black, the light which reaches it is absorbed, and little or none is reflected. By eliminating the light which before bounced off this back wall, the illumination at point "x" is reduced to 50 percent of its intensity in the case of the all-white room. The results of painting the other surfaces black are shown in the sequence of diagrams.

Figure 4-31 also shows similar comparisons for a room with a strip of windows across the back wall. In this case, the side walls and floor are more significant light reflectors than the back wall.

These figures, the results of actual tests, show that the *ceiling* is the most important surface in controlling the daylight coming into the room and reaching the task. Next in importance is the *back wall,* then the *side walls,* and finally the *floor*. This indicates at least two things to the designer: keep the ceiling as light in color as possible and use the floor surface for deep colors or character-giving patterns. Dark colors on the floor will have the least negative effect on the daylighting of tasks.

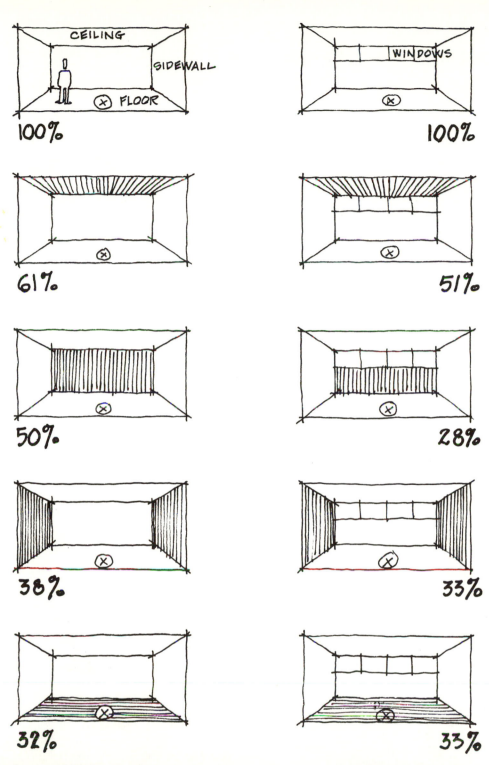

CEILING
SIDEWALL
FLOOR

WINDOWS

100%          100%

61%          51%

50%          28%

38%          33%

32%          33%

FIGURE 4-31. TESTS ON THE REDUCTION
OF LIGHTING AT POINT "X" DUE TO VARIOUS
BLACK-PAINTED WALLS SHOW WHICH SURFACES
ARE MOST EFFECTIVE IN SUPPORTING
TASK-LEVEL ILLUMINATION.

## Sloped Windows

Sloped windows or glass panes have seldom been thought to be particularly pertinent to daylighting design, but a word or two about the effect may be worthwhile. Sloped glass is most frequently used as a technique in street-side display cases or shop windows for eliminating viewable reflections on the glass. Vertical glass sometimes reflects images of brightly lighted objects in or across the street from behind the observer, which inhibits vision through the glass when the illumination in the showcase is less than that outside. Glass which is set back from the sidewalk at the bottom (sloping from top to bottom) will tend to reflect to the observer's eye an image of the flat sidewalk which is relatively uniform in texture and brightness and which is more easily shielded from sun and skylight by an overhang. The technique does not have significant advantages except, perhaps, in extreme cases.

The inwardly sloped glass has no effect on levels of daylight which reach the interior. The opaque material which supports the top of the glass may be considered as an overhang, which does affect the daylight contribution to the interior, but it is this and not the sloping of the glass which results in any change, as indicated in Figure 4-32.

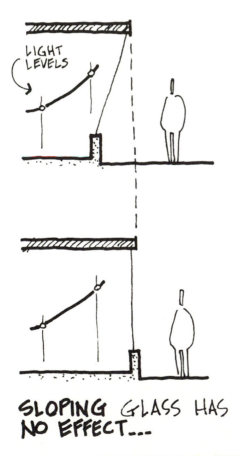

SLOPING GLASS HAS NO EFFECT...

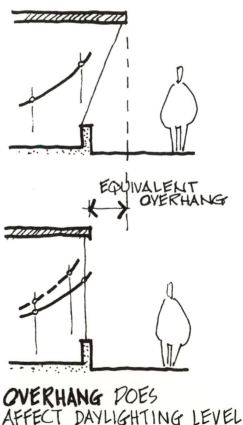

EQUIVALENT OVERHANG

OVERHANG DOES AFFECT DAYLIGHTING LEVEL

FIGURE 4-32. SLOPED-GLASS WINDOWS DO NOT AFFECT TASK-LEVEL ILLUMINATION, BUT THE "OVERHANG" DOES.

FIGURE 4-33.   While the geometry of the Dallas City Hall by architect I. M. Pei affects daylighting levels inside, the sloping glass does not have any significant effect.

I.M. Pei used sloping glass in the walls of his striking design for the new Dallas City Hall. While the geometry of the building shape does affect daylight levels inside, the sloping glass does not. The protruding overhead floor (and ceiling) increases the opportunities for ground-reflected light to reach the interior areas, but this would be the case regardless of the position of the glass. The sloping glass does, however, provide increased opportunities for a view of the ground area from the peripheral areas of the floors and certainly contributes to the over-all character of the building.

Outward-sloping glass, on the other hand, produces an effect somewhat like cutting the overhang back and allows significant quantities of daylight to penetrate the interior space. It also allows increased opportunities for viewing the exterior sky from inside, which usually creates excessive brightness ratios. The proposed design for the new TVA building in Chattanooga (still in the design stage) indicates sloped-glass areas on the north facade to allow extra penetration of daylight to the interior. However, since this glass area is visible only from the peripheral areas of the interior spaces, brightness controls were not a concern.

## DAYLIGHT CONTROLS

A variety of daylight controlling devices can be used which may be helpful in getting the daylight to where it is needed and for eliminating excessively bright areas from view. Some of these controls are dynamic (they can be moved) and some are static (they remain in place permanently). Dynamic controls have the advantage of allowing for change in response to changing sky conditions, thereby improving the efficiency of the design, but they have the disadvantage of requiring either an operator (usually the occupants—an unreliable source in general) or an expensive automatic device which can be difficult to main-

FIGURE 4-34. IN THE PRELIMINARY DESIGN FOR THE **TVA** BUILDING FOR CHATTANOOGA, TENNESSEE, **SLOPED** GLASS AND A **MIRROR** SURFACE ARE USED TO **BOUNCE** DAYLIGHT DEEP INTO THE INTERIOR.

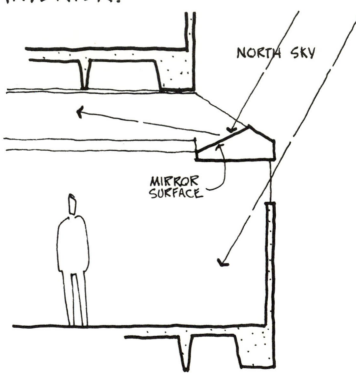

**TVA** OFFICE BUILDING
NORTH SIDE SECTION

tain. Static controls are less troublesome, but also less responsive and efficient.

**Reflecting Blinds, Louvers, and Shelves**
There are a variety of types of louvers for daylight control. They may be small, movable, and on the interior, such as venetian blinds; or they may be large and fixed on the exterior, as were commonly found on buildings built in the 1940s. Regardless of the type, they all perform basically the same way.

One of the most effective daylight controls are venetian blinds. They can be adjusted to exclude direct sunshine but to reflect its light to the ceiling where it will bounce into the interior areas of the space, while still allowing a view to the exterior; or they can be tilted to the closed position to essentially block all daylight and view.

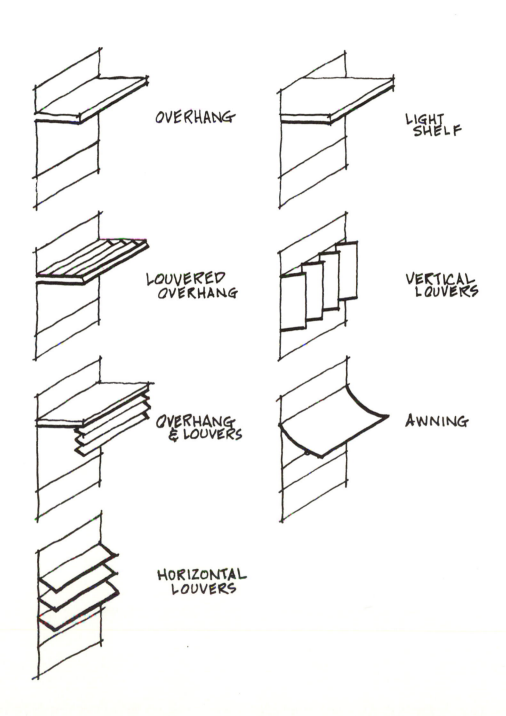

OVERHANG

LIGHT SHELF

LOUVERED OVERHANG

VERTICAL LOUVERS

OVERHANG & LOUVERS

AWNING

HORIZONTAL LOUVERS

## FIGURE 4-35. TYPES OF REFLECTOR/SHADES

FIGURE 4-36. PROPERLY ADJUSTED VENETIAN BLINDS REFLECT DAYLIGHT TO THE CEILING AND DO NOT PREVENT A VIEW TO THE EXTERIOR

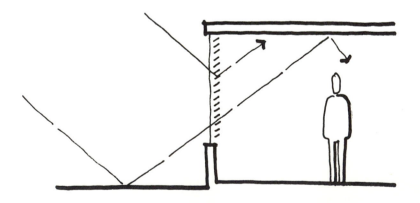

FIGURE 4-37. VENETIAN BLINDS TAKE ADVANTAGE OF REFLECTED GROUND LIGHT BY BOUNCING IT DEEP INTO THE INTERIOR OF THE SPACE

They can also be raised or lowered, and at the same time tilted, to control sun, sky brightness, and view. Venetian blinds have great versatility, and they tend to increase the ratio of the ground-reflected light to direct-sky contribution.

But they also have some disadvantages. For them to respond appropriately to changing sky conditions, they must be operated by a human operator with some understanding of the technology and the time and incentive to do the task. Venetian blinds tend to collect dirt and are tedious to clean. Their support straps are often unattractive and deteriorate over a few years. The control strings tend to be unsightly and sometimes get tangled and knotted. Nevertheless, they can be effective daylighting controls.

The Scandinavians have incorporated a thin, delicate venetian blind between two pieces of window glass, which eliminates the dirt-collection problem or, at least, transfers it from the blinds to the glass, and considerably simplifies the clumsiness of conventional blinds. To simplify maintenance, some of these types of windows have a removable or hinged sash. The English have produced a plastic shade with fine louvers stamped in the material to permit a view out while blocking the direct sun.

Horizontal louvers and overhangs are the most effective type of controls when the sun is high in the sky. They can be designed so as to allow entry of the warm winter sun and stop entry of the hot summer sun and they can also restrict view from the interior of exterior bright sky. One problem, however, of exterior louvers is that if the sunlighted surfaces of the louvers can be viewed from the interior, they may cause discomfort or disability or both because of their excessive brightness.

Vertical louvers are most effective for low sun angles such as occur early in the morning or late in the afternoon, or on building surfaces oriented to the east or west. For situations in which both the high sun and low sun must be considered, "egg-crate" louvers are often the most effective control since they combine the characteristics of both horizontal and vertical louvers.

FIGURE 4-38. Partially closed and lowered venetian blinds bounce daylight toward the ceiling and prevent a view to the bright outdoors.

FIGURE 4-39. Opening the blinds filters the daylight and sun and allows some view out.

FIGURE 4-40. Lifting the blinds partially allows a clear view out and also reflects daylight to the ceiling.

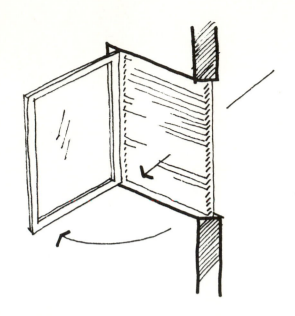

FIGURE 4-41. A TINY ADJUSTABLE BLIND BETWEEN TWO PANES OF GLASS REDUCES MAINTENANCE.

FIGURE 4-42. A PUNCHED, LOUVERED PLASTIC SHADE PREVENTS SUN PENETRATION AT MOST ANGLES.

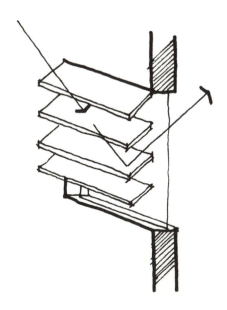

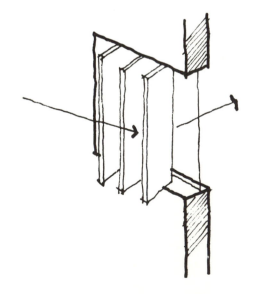

FIGURE 4-43. HORIZONTAL LOUVERS ARE EFFECTIVE WHEN THE SUN IS **HIGH** IN THE SKY (SOUTH-FACING WALL)

FIGURE 4-44. VERTICAL LOUVERS ARE EFFECTIVE WHEN THE SUN IS **LOW** IN THE SKY (WEST-FACING WALL)

For a high-rise, speculative office building design for a major southwestern city, where the faces of the structure were to be oriented to the southeast and northwest, egg-crate louvers were recommended for preventing direct sun penetration. For these orientations, neither horizontal nor vertical louvers alone would effectively prevent sun penetration. The design which evolved, based on a very stringent budget and the particular circumstances of the job, is shown in Figure 4-45. To get as much daylight as possible with direct sun penetration, small egg-crate louvers will be sandwiched between the two planes of clear glass across the top of the fenestration of each floor. The egg-crate louvers will block the sun but reflect daylight into the space, and at the same time prevent a view of the bright sky from the interior. The center section of the double-glass fenestration wall is tinted via a chemical pigment in the inner-side of the outer layer of the glass, which allows a view to the exterior, but reduces exterior brightnesses and direct sun. The lower section of the fenestration is opaque.

## Skylight and Roof Reflectors

Direct sunshine is so intense a source of light and heat that its direct penetration into building spaces generally creates problems. The conventional techniques for avoiding these problems, so far as roof openings are concerned, is to use some kind of louver, shade, or translucent material on the interior of the opening, thereby reflecting, diffusing, and/or reducing the quantity of light (and heat) that penetrates. But exterior controls are much more effective than interior controls in eliminating the undesirable effects of the sun while still allowing use of its desirable effects.

For each unit of light in the interior (by whatever unit of measurement), more radiant heat is transmitted to the interior with direct sun than with diffuse radiation from the sky where much of the sun's longer infrared energy waves are lost. Thus, it is advantageous, whenever possible, to intercept the direct sun before it gets inside.

With plastic-dome skylights, the recommendation is usually for a low-transmission, translucent plastic to reduce the radiant heat and diffuse the light. But a much better solution would be to use a transparent

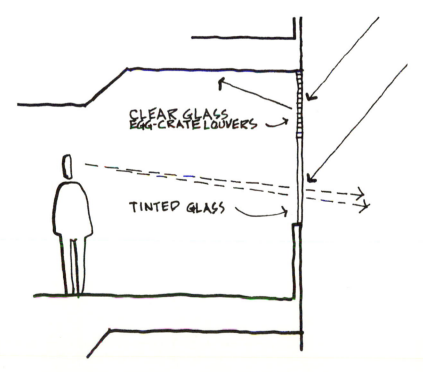

FIGURE 4-45. EGG-CRATE LOUVERS REFLECT DAYLIGHT IN --- TINTED GLASS ALLOWS VISION TO THE OUTSIDE

FIGURE 4-46. These egg-crate overhangs were used in the Harvard Undergraduate Science Center by architect Josep Lluis Sert for sun control.

FIGURE 4-47. Exterior view of egg-crate overhangs used in the Harvard Undergraduate Science Center.

glazing material with a sun shade on the exterior. Such a shade as shown in Figure 4-48 could effectively shade the skylight from the sun during warm weather periods, just as overhangs shade vertical openings, and allow penetration during the cold season. Or, if it were desirable, this type of shade could keep the direct sun off the skylight and, hence, out of the interior, all year around. There are many advantages to using an exterior shade: a clear skylight with exterior shading could be smaller than the more typical diffuse skylight with no shading; capital cost savings from the reduced size of the skylight could be applied to the cost of the exterior shading device; and the reduction in the radiant heat contribution to the interior during the cooling season would reduce cooling costs considerably. The disadvantages are, of course, the added cost of the shading device, the possible maintenance required (although that might be minimal), and the need for some knowledgeable person to design the shade to have the proper shading characteristics.

Similar shading devices can be used for other types of roof openings. I.M. Pei's design for the Dallas Municipal Center utilizes clerestories which face to the north sky, but which benefit from the light reflected from the exterior of the concrete vault of the adjacent clerestory. The result is a beautiful, soft-lighted, vaulted ceiling (see Figure 4-49).

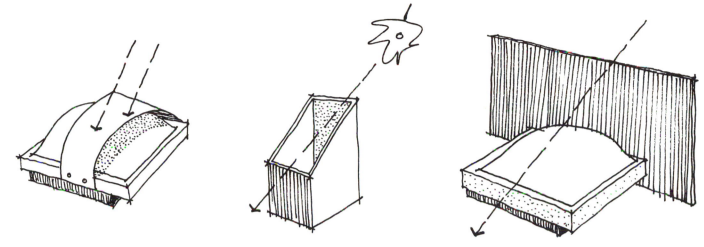

FIGURE 4-48. SKYLIGHT SHADES CAN HELP KEEP THE **HEAT** OUT DURING THE **HOTTEST** PART OF THE DAY, BUT STILL ALLOW **PLENTY** OF **DAYLIGHT**.

FIGURE 4-49. Light is reflected off the backside of clerestories and parapet walls to bounce into the interior of the Dallas City Hall.

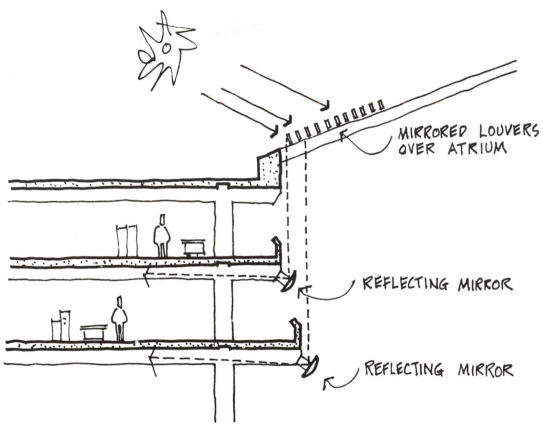

MIRRORED LOUVERS OVER ATRIUM

REFLECTING MIRROR

REFLECTING MIRROR

FIGURE 4-50. SUNLIGHT IS REFLECTED BY MIRRORS IN THE PROPOSED NEW TVA BUILDING

Such design techniques are often in many ways more daylighting-effective than some of the more common exterior types of louvers and do not have the same inherent maintenance problems, such as bird and insect infestation.

The proposed design for the TVA Building for Chattanooga, Tennessee, utilizes, over the atrium skylight, operable exterior louvers. These will continuously track the sun, redirecting sunlight into or out of the atrium as necessary to control heat and light, and, at the same time, allow diffuse or reflected light to enter. The louvers are mirrored on one side to reflect direct sun, and diffuse-white on the other side to reflect and diffuse light from the sky. The louvers are to be automatically rotated as the sun moves or repositioned at set intervals. They can be closed at night to eliminate heat loss from nighttime radiation to the sky. Experience will prove whether or not the cost of operation and maintenance of this sophisticated system will be practical and cost-effective. The concept is certainly on target.

## Mirrors and Polished Reflectors

The TVA Building just described is one of the few real examples of attempts to use mirrors to reflect light deep into the interior of a building. The principal difference in reflecting the light via mirrors rather than with diffuse reflecting surfaces is in the intensity and directness of the projected light. A mirror reflects a very high percentage of the light which strikes it and, therefore, any object, surface, or person which intercepts this light is effectively being exposed to the real, direct sun or sky. The mirror as a source then, must be dealt with much as the direct sun and sky. This mirror-reflected light may cause excessive brightness on the surfaces it strikes unless properly utilized. Visual contact with the reflected sun or even the clear or cloudy sky through the mirror may result in interior brightness problems.

Experiments have also been performed with polished reflectors on the back side of venetian blinds. When the blinds are properly adjusted, the light is reflected into the interior positions of the room, which produces a level of intensity at desk height slightly higher than with the conventional white venetian blind slats. Keeping mirrored blinds "properly adjusted" can be, of course, a problem in itself.

Horizontal shelves equipped with mirrors or polished metal can also be an effective technique for increasing the daylight contribution to a space. Again, care must be exercised to be sure that the resulting brightness patterns will not be objectionable.

## Drapes and Fine Screens

Drapes are among the architect's favorite control devices because they add beauty and color, texture, and "softness" to a space, with considerable flexibility. Fabrics are available which provide a range of openness of weave and reflectivity of surface to fulfill a variety of requirements. They can provide a complete blackout or just about any degree of light transmission desired. Drapes which are effectively translucent will present some of the same problems as the translucent panels discussed earlier. If exposed to direct sun, their surface brightness can be a problem, but, of

FIGURE 4-51. This photo of the inside of a model used by W.C. Lam in studying the design of the Chattanooga TVA building shows how the mirrored shelves across the atrium openings will reflect daylight into interior spaces.

FIGURE 4-52. Drapes can be effective and attractive daylight controls.

FIGURE 4-53. Trees outside the New England Center for Continuing Education delightfully filter incoming sun and daylight.

course, they can be withdrawn. Often, the interior visual conditions are more favorable with direct sun coming into the room, rather than with the sun-lighted translucent drapes. More flexibility can be achieved through the use of two separately tracked drapes over the same opening. One drape may be used to reduce light entry, while the use of the second can completely block out the daylight.

Control elements inside the room, such as drapes and blinds, absorb heat, especially when exposed to direct sun. Some of this heat is reflected back out, but most is released into the interior space by convection to the air and by radiation to objects in the room.

There are several types of slated or stamped metal screens on the market which are quite effective for sun and sky shading and for reflecting daylight into the interior of buildings. These screens employ minute slats (as small as 0.05 inches) spaced so closely together (17 to 23 louvers per inch) that they prevent the passage of all but the tiniest insects while still allowing vision through. The minute slats are tilted at a slight angle (about 17 degrees) to the horizontal, so that they provide sun control at sun angles of about 25 degrees and above. These screens are fabricated to resist deterioration, and at least one company manufacturers a roll-up screen.

## Filtering Daylight with Vegetation

Trees, shrubs, and hanging vines are excellent items for use in filtering daylight into building spaces. Louis Kahn used vegetation to filter and soften daylight in the Kimbell Art Museum (see Figures 8–20 and 21). He also used trimmed trees to form an umbrella over the entrance path to facilitate eye-adaption upon entering the building. Trees outside windows are excellent devices for blocking view of the excessively bright sky (see Figure 8–16). Hanging vines on the interior of clerestories and skylights provide a good filtering device, but, of course, they require maintenance.

## GLAZING MATERIALS

While the efficiency of electric lighting equipment is increasing in response to the demand for energy conservation and to the rising price of energy, so, too, is the efficiency of daylight increasing in the sense that window glazing materials are being developed which will allow greater control of light and heat transmission. Referred to as "selectively-transmitting," these materials permit the passage of some parts of the radiant energy spectrum (light), while reflecting or absorbing other parts (heat producing). All glazing materials (glass, plastic, etc.) are to some degree selectively-transmitting. For instance, 1/8-inch clean, clear glass transmits about 90 percent of the visible energy which strikes it, while allowing only about 79 percent of the infrared (heat-producing) radiant energy to pass through.

But there are new materials being developed which will allow a much greater percentage of light than infrared transmission. In time, these new materials will add a measurable increase in the efficiency and cost-effectiveness of daylighting, and their use will become common practice. Those selectively-transmitting materials which are available now have somewhat limited applicability, and all have some shortcomings as daylighting mediums.

## Tinted

The tinted, transparent glasses and plastics are probably the most common types of selectively-transmitting materials in use now. They allow a view out but restrict the amount of daylight and sun that comes in. They are produced principally in gray and bronze, or variations thereof, although they are available in other colors. The gray materials are neutral so that interior colors are rendered realistically, but colored transparent materials will distort the appearance of interior colors and should be avoided. Light transmittances of these tinted materials ranges from the very dark (10 to 15 percent) to the very light (70 to 80 percent), and their transmittance of the infrared spectrum (heat-producing) is only slightly more restricted—usually 10 to 15 percent below that of the visible transmittance.

With such tinted materials, the view out is not noticeably affected during the day, except with the use of very low-transmittance materials, which sometimes are quite no-

FIGURE 4-54. Tinted glass can be effective in reducing exterior brightness, but at the expense of greatly reduced daylighting.

FIGURE 4-55. Tinted glass viewed from the outside may appear quite opaque in the daytime.

FIGURE 4-56. These translucent panels reduce exterior brightnesses when they are in the shade, but when they are in direct sun, become excessively bright.

ticeable and often produce the feeling that it is going to rain. Even the lighter transmittance materials will produce this "gloomy" feeling when exterior light levels are quite low, such as just before darkness. Some glazing materials are treated so as to reflect (rather than transmit or absorb) through the application of metallic or metallic oxide coatings or films, and their transmittance properties vary widely with the manufacturer. These tinted and reflective materials have a tendency to reduce the view into the interior from outdoors, which some people find frustrating. During night hours, when the electric lights are burning inside, the opposite occurs—people can see in but not out.

## Translucent

Glazing materials, such as opal and surface-treated glasses, diffusing and patterned plastics and glasses, corrugated plastics and glasses, and diffusing glass block, are light-transmitting but translucent —they do not permit a view through. The amount of light diffusion varies from slight diffusion spread over a small angle, to complete diffusion spread over a wide angle. Generally, transmittance decreases as diffusion increases.

A majority of the plastic-dome type of skylights are used with translucent plastics. Most of these diffusing materials become excessively bright with exposure to the sun, so they should not be used where they may be seen from interior visual task areas. As mentioned before, since they prevent direct penetration of the sun as well as view to the exterior, their value in satisfying biological needs is minimal. They should be used only in special circumstances when their characteristics and the resulting environment are clearly understood and appropriate.

## Directional Transmitting

Some glazing materials produce a definite, controlled change in the direction of the transmitted light by refraction. The light-directing glass block is the most familiar of these, although some plastics and prismatic glasses may be classified as directional. The light-directing glass block employs prisms on the two faces to get the

FIGURE 4-57. Diffusing materials often create excessive brightness and seldom satisfy the biological need to see out.

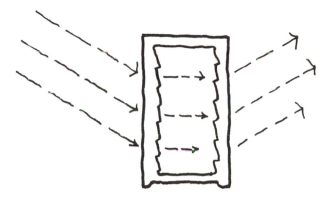

FIGURE 4-58. PRISMATIC GLASS BLOCK REDIRECTS DAYLIGHT TOWARD THE INTERIOR CEILING

FIGURE 4-59. This glass-block skylight provides an ample supply of daylight. Open areas at the ends of the mall allow shoppers to maintain contact with the exterior.

desired directional control. Some are designed for vertical installation, as in the fenestration of a school room, and some for horizontal installation in skylights. They are used primarily to reflect daylight onto the ceiling of a room to increase light levels deep in the interior and to eliminate the bright sky from view, or in the case of skylights, to transmit light while maintaining a reasonably low surface brightness even when exposed to direct sun. Glass block is designed to restrict the brightness seen from normal viewing angles. This directional characteristic, of course, also prevents clear vision through, and so, in a sense, limits the satisfaction of biological needs.

FIGURE 4-60.   Clear glass block in this Houston art school produces a unique daylighted atmosphere.

A rather unique application of *clear* glass block can be seen in the Alfred C. Glanell, Jr. School of Art building in Houston, designed by S.I. Morris. The entire exterior curtain wall consists of clear glass block which allows an ample contribution of daylight to the interior, but which has a very good resistance to convected heat. The transparent block permits vision to the exterior, although objects appear somewhat distorted and vision from outside in is likewise restricted.

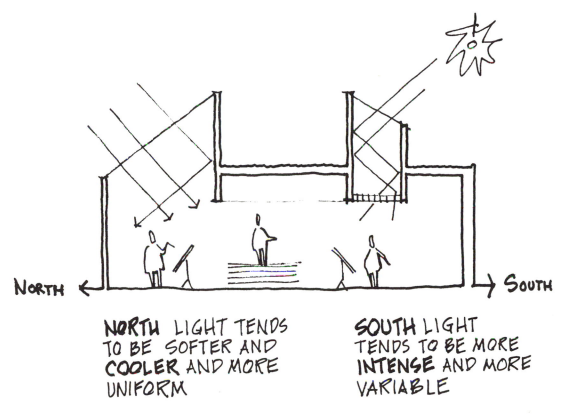

NORTH ←        → SOUTH

NORTH LIGHT TENDS
TO BE SOFTER AND
COOLER AND MORE
UNIFORM

SOUTH LIGHT
TENDS TO BE MORE
INTENSE AND MORE
VARIABLE

FIGURE 4-61. ___BUT ORIENTATION OF THE
BUILDING HAS LITTLE EFFECT ON THE QUALITY
OF INTERIOR DAYLIGHT IF DIRECT SUN IS
PROPERLY CONTROLLED.

## ORIENTATION

In so far as daylighting is concerned, any building orientation can be adapted to provide good interior lighting. There is nothing significantly different about the daylight that comes from the north, south, east, or west except as related to the geometry of the sun's motion across the sky. Traditionally, building spaces oriented toward the north sky have been considered the most desirable for producing good visual conditions, and the romanticized artist in the mind's eye is always working in a studio with a large and sloping window facing to the north. Except for a slight variation in color spectrum, which is for most purposes insignificant, the light from the north sky is no different from that of the south, east, or west sky, except in intensity and contribution from the direct sun. Orientation is primarily a factor in dealing with the direct sun. The same soft, diffuse daylight condition that comes from the north sky can be achieved with any other orientation and intelligent use of proper daylight controls.

# 5

# THE NATURE OF THE SKIES

The changing nature of the sky is one of its most valuable assets. Its constantly changing variety, beauty, and excitement provides humankind with countless joys. These qualities transmitted into building interiors assist people in maintaining a continuing relationship between nature and the subtle biological forces at work in the subconscious mind. But it is this same changing nature of the sky which creates some frustration and confusion when it comes to quantifying daylighting conditions in buildings.

A thorough understanding of the basic principles of daylighting design is essentially all that the capable designer needs in order to produce a well-daylighted building. If the fundamentals are applied, the result will be successful. A model study or a few calculations can be used to compare alternative designs and to indicate whether the design will produce some acceptable level of illumination under some specified sky condition. Selecting the best design from a variety of otherwise acceptable possibilities is the first goal. But the question is, "How do we know what kind of sky conditions we are going to have at the site and how does that relate to the building design?"

## SKY CONDITIONS

The luminance or brightness of the sky changes almost constantly, although the changes are often not discernible by the human eye. The sun's changing position in the sky is the principal factor in the process, but particles of moisture (clouds), dust, and pollution in the air also have an effect. Some clear days (without discernible clouds) are clearer than others. Some overcast days are more overcast (thicker clouds) than others. Oftentimes, moisture high in the sky and not visible to the eye will alter the amount of daylight reaching the ground. Thus, the illumination level on the ground is in a constant state of change. It will be helpful to the designer to have an understanding of the three basic types of skies and their resulting effect on building conditions.

## The Overcast Sky

The dense, overcast sky is the most uniform type of sky condition and generally tends to change more slowly than other types of skies. The overcast sky is defined by the Weather Service as being a sky in which at least 9/10 of the total sky is visually obscured by clouds. The overcast sky has a general luminance distribution that is about three times brighter at the zenith than at the horizon. This is the type of sky most often considered for daylighting studies (almost exclusively in England and Europe) and is usually considered the minimum daylighting condition that will be experienced in the full-scale building. However, the illumination produced by the overcast sky on the earth's surface may vary from several hundred footcandles to several thousand, depending on the den-

THE OVERCAST SKY

- DIFFUSE
- BRIGHT
- STEADY

FIGURE 5-1. THE OVERCAST SKY MAY BE DARK OR BRIGHT, BUT IS USUALLY BRIGHT AND PRODUCES A DIFFUSE LIGHT OF VARYING INTENSITY.

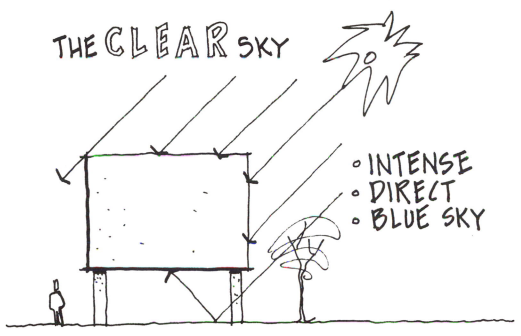

FIGURE 5-2. THE CLEAR SKY WITH DIRECT SUN PRODUCES AN INTENSE, DIRECT LIGHT WITH A RELATIVELY DARK (BLUE) SKY.

sity of the clouds. Vision of the overcast sky from within a building will usually be undesirable, because of the contrast between the higher brightness of the sky and the lowered levels of brightness inside. Unfortunately, a design which works well under the "minimum" condition of an overcast sky will not necessarily work well under a bright sun, so that the overcast sky should not be used as the only condition to be considered.

## The Clear Sky with Sunshine

The clear sky, disregarding the direct sun for the moment, is less bright than the overcast sky and tends to be brighter at the horizon than at the zenith. It tends to be fairly stable in luminance except for the area surrounding the sun which, of course, changes as the sun moves. The total level of illumination produced by the clear sky and sun varies constantly, but slowly, throughout the day. Many so-called clear skies are, in fact, loaded with moisture that affects the amount of light that penetrates and causes illumination levels to fluctuate. Depending on the geographic location and local atmospheric conditions, the illumination levels produced can range from 5000 to 12,000 footcandles. Most daylighting study techniques are based on the presumption that no direct sunlight will penetrate the building fenestration, for the simple reason that direct sun on the interior is considered to produce undesirable seeing conditions, particularly if direct sun reaches visual tasks such as desks and chalkboards. Therefore, there are no calculation techniques available for predicting interior lighting levels when direct sunshine is present. Only scale-model studies will provide this information.

### The Partly Cloudy Sky

The partly cloudy sky has a cloud cover that may range from quite heavy to very light. It can vary greatly in terms of sky (or cloud) luminance; it usually includes widely varying luminances from one area of the sky to another; and it tends to change quite rapidly. In addition, the partly cloudy sky may provide periods when direct sun will reach the building site and some periods when, for all practical purposes, the sky is as if overcast. The partly cloudy sky, when the sun penetrates directly to the building site, will provide the highest level of illumination as well as the brightest visual impact (white clouds) from within the building.

## QUANTIFYING AVAILABLE DAYLIGHT

A close look at the weather data for a specific locality will indicate the general day-

THE PARTLY CLOUDY SKY

- INTENSE
- BRIGHT SKY
- CHANGING

FIGURE 5-3. THE PARTLY CLOUDY SKY PROVIDES BOTH INTENSE AND DIFFUSE LIGHT, USUALLY WITH EXCESSIVELY BRIGHT CLOUDS IN CHANGING PATTERNS.

light conditions to be expected. If the climate is generally cold, the building design can tolerate a greater percent of direct sun. If the climate is generally hot, direct sun will not be very welcome, but there will be plenty of daylight to work with. If the climate has a high percent of possible sunshine, the building design can be focused on high exterior intensity levels and the overcast sky can be downplayed. If the climate is frequently overcast, the designer will have to focus on larger openings for daylight and brightness control and downplay the bright, sunny days. This is not to say that the sunny day, in this case, should be ignored, but for this climate, it is less significant a consideration.

If, however, we are to quantify daylight, for instance, to determine what percent of daylight hours certain electric lights may be turned off as an energy-conserving measure, we face a quandary. We will want to know how much light there is outside at our site and how long it will remain at certain levels. If we have determined, for instance, that with a particular building design we will get 30 footcandles at some point inside when the illumination on the vertical face of the building is 2400 footcandles, making it possible, at that point, to turn off the electric lights, we will want to know how many hours of the day that exterior illumination level will be above 2400 footcandles. If the conditions are known, the saved energy and the associated costs or savings can be quantified.

But there is almost no data available on how much daylight there is throughout the year at various places across the country. Measurements over the seasons have been made at only a few locations in the United States. Unless you are designing for Ann Arbor, Port Allegheny, Washington, D.C., or San Francisco, complete data will not be available, and the data for San Francisco has yet to be published.[1]

There are graphs (see Figure 5-8) which provide some indication of the possible daylight both on horizontal and vertical surfaces, according to solar altitude and type of sky condition (e.g., overcast, clear summer sky, clear autumn/spring sky, and clear winter sky). These charts are highly theoretical and translating them successfully into meaningful figures for a specific locality is questionable at best, but they are the only means available outside of actual local measurements.[2]

The National Oceanic and Atmospheric Administration of the Department of Commerce publishes useful weather data through the National Climatic Center on percent of cloud cover and possible sunshine at stations throughout the United States.[3] The Weather Bureau observers estimate the degree of cloudiness as tenths of the entire sky: 0/10 to 3/10 being clear, 4/10 to 7/10 partly cloudy, and 8/10 to 10/10 cloudy. Although this data is obviously very approximate, it can be useful in estimating the number of hours that exterior illumination will be above certain levels.

The Weather Bureau is now measuring and recording both diffuse and direct solar radiation levels at selected stations across the country, and some attempts have been made to transpose insolation data into illumination data, but with only very limited success. At this point in time, not enough is known about the technique to extend application beyond these initial, but specific, exercises.

With the extremely limited data on available daylight illumination, it is not possible to accurately predict absolute values of interior daylight levels or to make the desired definitive life cycle cost-benefit analyses. Thus, attempts to quantify energy savings and other cost savings accrued from daylighting become highly theoretical.

However, absolute values, either in footcandles or dollars, are not as important as comparing design alternatives, and alternatives can be compared using almost any index. But if we are to evaluate design alternatives of daylight versus electric light, in which the latter involves rather specific absolute values, then we must have some absolutes for daylight that will provide the basis for comparison. The lack of data on daylight availability puts economic and energy comparisons on rather shaky ground and increases the need for designers to be persuasive if they want to use daylight.

We are then left with a dilemma: "What are we to use as a basis for determining interior daylight contributions?" On the basis of the analysis just offered, one can see that some type of standard, reasonably well-accepted database will have to suffice. The only database presently available would seem to be charts such as those in Figure 5-5 or those in the IES Recommended Practice of Daylighting, a document that was revised in 1979 by the IES Daylighting Committee. These charts were empirically derived, based on several research efforts over the past 50 to 60 years and represent, probably, the best general sun and sky illumination information available. The charts can be supplemented by local weather data and a little common sense to provide a reasonable basis for daylight availability estimates.

**An Example:**

There are probably a number of ways to approach this problem, but here is one suggestion. Let's assume an office-building design which model studies have shown will provide a level of 30 footcandles of illumination on the interior to a distance of 15 feet away from the window wall when the illumination on the vertical, south-facing building surface is 2400 footcandles. The fenestration is so designed that no direct sun can penetrate to the interior. The building is occupied for nine hours each day, 8 A.M. to 5 P.M., five days each week, and four weeks per month. Its location is outside Lynchburg, Virginia (36° north latitude; 79° longitude west). When the interior illumination level is above 30 footcandles, a bank of six luminaires need not be illuminated. Below 30 footcandles, they will need to be turned on and will then consume electricity. How much energy would be saved annually with the use of this quantity of daylight?

From Weather Bureau data, in Lynchburg, 40 percent of the days are cloudy (8/10 to 10/10 overcast), 29 percent are partly cloudy days, and 31 percent are clear days (between sunrise and sunset). (See Figure 5-5.) With a sun angle calculator (see Figure 5-6), the true altitude of the sun and angle (or azimuth) between the sun and the south face of the building can be determined for each hour between 8 A.M. and 5 P.M. and plotted as shown in Figure 5-7 (typical for one hour only).

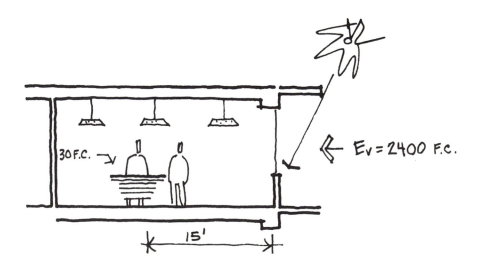

FIGURE 5-4. LYNCHBURG, VIRGINIA HYPOTHETICAL BUILDING

## CLIMATOGRAPHY OF THE U.S. No. 60-44
### CLIMATES OF THE STATES (VIRGINIA)
## NORMALS, MEANS, AND EXTREMES

| | PERCENT POSSIBLE SUN | MEAN SKY COVER SUNRISE-SUNSET | MEAN NUMBER OF DAYS SUNRISE TO SUNSET | | |
|---|---|---|---|---|---|
| | | | CLEAR | PARTLY CLOUDY | CLOUDY |
| J | 51% | 6.2 | 9 | 7 | 15 |
| F | 55 | 6.1 | 8 | 7 | 13 |
| M | 58 | 6.0 | 9 | 9 | 13 |
| A | 59 | 6.1 | 8 | 9 | 13 |
| M | 63 | 6.0 | 8 | 11 | 12 |
| J | 66 | 5.7 | 8 | 12 | 10 |
| J | 61 | 5.9 | 7 | 12 | 12 |
| A | 61 | 5.8 | 8 | 12 | 11 |
| S | 63 | 5.3 | 11 | 8 | 11 |
| O | 62 | 4.7 | 14 | 7 | 10 |
| N | 56 | 5.5 | 11 | 7 | 12 |
| D | 53 | 5.8 | 11 | 6 | 14 |
| YR. | 59 | 5.8 | 112 | 107 | 146 |
| | | | (31%) | (29%) | (40%) |

FIGURE 5-5. A portion of Weather Bureau data for the Lynchburg, Virginia, area.

FIGURE 5-6. One plate from the excellent Libbey-Owens-Ford "Sun Angle Calculator," available from the Libbey-Owens-Ford Company, 811 Madison Avenue, Toledo, Ohio.

Copyright © 1974 Libbey-Owens-Ford Company

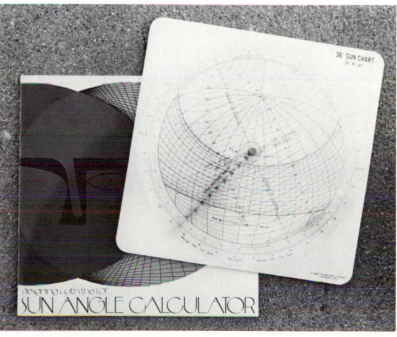

### 8:00 A.M.

| | | TRUE ALTITUDE | AZIMUTH | F.C. (SKY) | F.C. (SUN) | F.C. TOTAL |
|---|---|---|---|---|---|---|
| WINTER | DEC 21 | 7° | 53° | 475 | 1000 | 1475 |
| WINTER | JAN 21 | 10° | 55° | 500 | 1800 | 2300 |
| SPRING AUTUMN | FEB 21 | 17° | 62° | 650 | 2000 | 2650 |
| SPRING AUTUMN | MAR 21 | 24° | 71° | 710 | 1900 | 2610 |
| SPRING AUTUMN | APR 21 | 31° | 81° | 660 | 1300 | 1960 |
| SUMMER | MAY 21 | 36° | 90° | 680 | — | 680 |
| SUMMER | JUN 21 | 37° | 93° | 650 | — | 650 |

FIGURE 5-7. Exterior footcandle levels on the vertical for one hour of the day (typical).

Then, from the illumination curves (Figure 5–8), the illumination on the vertical south-facing wall of the building can be determined for each of the four sky conditions. The average monthly illumination values on the south-facing wall can then be graphed as shown in Figure 5–9. Figure 5–9 indicates there are 24 month-hour periods when the illumination on the vertical face of the building will be below 2400 footcandles. Multiplied by 20 days per month-hour, the total is 480 hours below 2400 footcandles, or 1680 hours above, for a year of 100 percent clear days.

According to the Weather Bureau data, Lynchburg has 40 percent cloudy (overcast) days.[5] The illumination curves (Figure 5–8) for overcast skies show that illumination on the vertical face of the building will always be below 2400 footcandles on overcast days. Thus, subtracting 40 percent of the 1680 remaining hours, leaves 1008 hours of clear sky with illumination levels on the vertical above 2400 footcandles.

The Weather Bureau data also indicates 29 percent partly cloudy days. Arbitrarily assuming that one-half the hours during partly cloudy days will be below 2400 footcandles, and one-half above, the 1008 clear-sky hour figure is multiplied by .29 and again by .50.

The result is 862 hours per year when the illumination on the vertical face will be above 2400 footcandles and the lights may be turned off, and 1298 hours when the spaces will have to be electrically lighted. This data can then be used to calculate the energy savings due to the perimeter electric lights being turned off. In figuring total costs, window heat losses and gains in the winter and gains in the summer must also be determined.

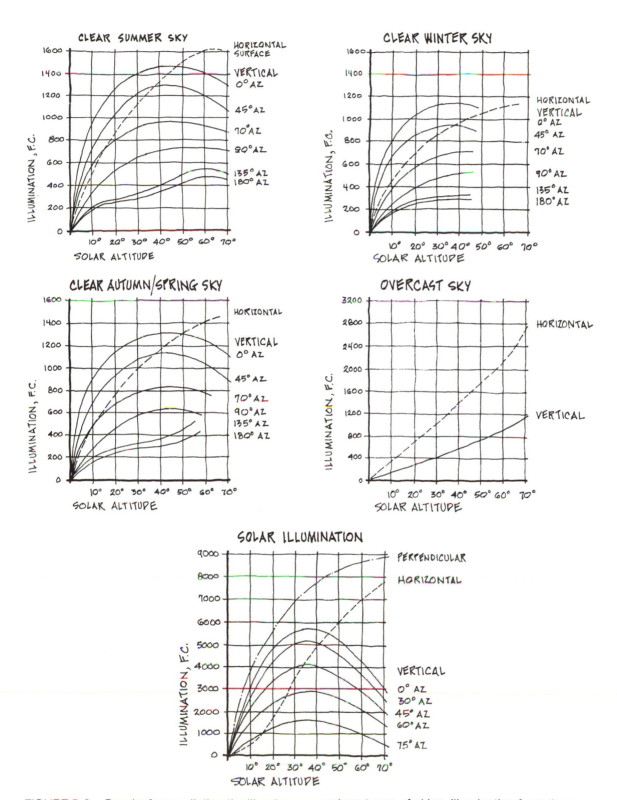

FIGURE 5-8.  Graphs for predicting the illumination on the horizontal and vertical surfaces under various types of skies. Illumination from the sun is considered separately.

# LYNCHBURG, VIRGINIA
## CLEAR SKY — FOOTCANDLES ON THE VERTICAL

| | A.M. | | | | | P.M. | | | |
|------|------|------|-------|-------|-------|------|------|------|------|
| | 8:00 | 9:00 | 10:00 | 11:00 | 12:00 | 1:00 | 2:00 | 3.00 | 4.00 |
| DEC | 1475 | 4060 | 5660 | 6380 | 6760 | | | | |
| JAN | 2300 | 4390 | 5570 | 6480 | 6820 | | | | |
| FEB | 2650 | 3950 | 5740 | 6520 | 6720 | | | | |
| MAR | 2610 | 3750 | 5130 | 5200 | 5900 | | | | |
| APR | 1960 | 3030 | 3600 | 4680 | 4450 | | | | |
| MAY | 680 | 1640 | 2600 | 3000 | 3100 | | | | |
| JUN | 650 | 1400 | 2200 | 2700 | 2450 | | | | |
| JUL | 680 | 1640 | 2600 | 3000 | 3100 | | | | |
| AUG | 1960 | 3030 | 3600 | 4680 | 4450 | | | | |
| SEP | 2610 | 3750 | 5130 | 5200 | 5900 | | | | |
| OCT | 2650 | 3950 | 5740 | 6520 | 6720 | | | | |
| NOV | 2300 | 4390 | 5570 | 6480 | 6820 | | | | |

SYMMETRICAL

FOOTCANDLES BELOW 2400

FIGURE 5-9. Daylight levels on the vertical surface of the building by hour and month.

# FIGURE 5-10. STEPS IN CALCULATING ANTICIPATED ILLUMINATION LEVELS.

## 1. ANNUAL HOURS OF OPERATION

12 MOS X 4 WEEKS/MO X 5 DAYS/WK X 9 HOURS/DAY = 2160 HRS/YR

## 2. ILLUMINATION ON VERTICAL BELOW 2400 FOOTCANDLES

24 MONTH-HOUR PERIODS X 20 WEEKS/YR = 480 HRS/YR

## 3. VERTICAL ILLUMINATION ABOVE 2400 FOOTCANDLES

2160 − 480 = 1680 HRS/YR

## 4. HOURS LOST UNDER OVERCAST SKY

1680 − (40% X 1680) = 1008 HRS/YR REMAINING

## 5. HOURS LOST FOR PARTLY CLOUDY DAYS

1008 − (29% X 50% X 1008) = **862** HRS/YR REMAINING

# EVALUATION OF DESIGN ALTERNATIVES WITH MODELS

There are a variety of techniques available to the architect for simulating the daylighting performance of buildings. Mathematical methods were developed in the 1920s by Moon and Spencer[1] and others, which allowed for calculation of task illumination based on a known sky and given geometry of structure. Later, these mathematical processes were adapted for computer use by O'Brien[2], DiLaura[3], and others. As useful as these mathematical processes can be, they have some rather severe limitations: the mathematics are exceedingly complex and, therefore, the range of room shapes and sizes and architectural details that can be accommodated are limited.

There are also several graphic methods for calculating daylight. In general, these methods employ some type of protractor or overlay with predetermined lines and patterns which, when used on an appropriate scale drawing, provide quite simple and satisfactory results for certain limited conditions. These graphic methods have been developed by researchers in England, France, and Australia[4], but are, unfortunately, not readily available in America.

These, too, are limited to use with relatively simple architectural designs.

The most widely used prediction method in America is the one published by the Illuminating Engineering Society (IES)[5] which is based on empirical data developed by Griffith[6] and which employs the same basic lumen method used for predetermining electric lighting levels. Again, while the method is extremely useful for buildings whose dimensions and conditions are suitable, it is limited to a relatively narrow range of architectural conditions which restrict its application and detract from its accuracy.

Finally, there is the *model* simulation process which provides the simplest, most versatile, and most reliable technique for studying the daylighting of a building while it is still in the design stage.

## MODEL STUDIES

The physics of illumination is such that light behaves exactly the same way in a model as it does in a full-scale building. If the scale model is a duplicate of the full-scale building in all respects and if it is tested under identical sky conditions, the results in the model will be identical to those of the full-scale building. The feasibility of using models for daylighting studies has been well established by scientists in this country[7] and in Europe.[8]

Model simulation may be conducted under an actual sky or in a simulated sky where conditions can be held constant. A number of successful attempts have been made to develop simulated skies for use with models, notably at Texas A & M College in the 1950s*, and in England, Europe, and Australia. The simulated sky provides opportunity for model tests under non-varying sky conditions, which is a great advantage. Unfortunately, such facilities are too costly except for institutions such as universities and research laboratories. Simulated skies are presently in use in America at Virginia Polytechnic Institute and State University, Blacksburg; at the University of Washington, Seattle; and at the University of California at Berkeley, and

FIGURE 6-1. The environmental laboratory at Texas A & M, 1950–60, with the simulated sky (large dome in background).

*The dome at Texas A & M is no longer in use.

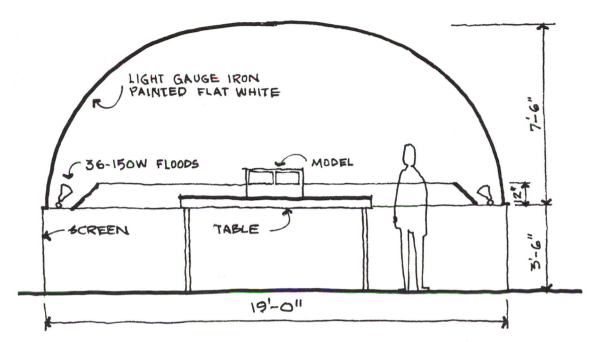

FIGURE 6-2. CROSS SECTION OF THE SIMULATED SKY AT **TEXAS A&M** WHICH WAS DISMANTLED IN 1963.

for those who have access to these facilities, their use can be quite beneficial.

However, while simulated skies are not always available, model studies under normal sky conditions, which are available to us all, can yield worthwhile results. Model studies under the real sky involve no complicated math or other maneuvers with which the average architect cannot cope. Model building is a routine activity in the offices of most architects and only slight modifications to this normal practice are usually necessary for using these models for daylight studies. The instrumentation required for quantitative measurements is simple, if not inexpensive. The opportunity for qualitative evaluation through visual observation and photography enhances the use of models.

However, any simulation process has limitations and while, in theory, models can exactly reproduce the daylighting conditions of the full-scale building, it is not always feasible or possible to build the model exactly as the full-scale building. Also, it is not always possible to determine what type of sky or skies the full-scale building will experience or to conduct model studies under similar skies. Instruments do not always measure just what the eye would see, and those who test models and wield instruments do not always measure correctly. If these limitations are recognized and understood, model studies can be useful in producing meaningful results.

There are several things that can be accomplished through model studies. First, even very crude models can provide an *approximation* of the illumination levels that will result from a basic design scheme. If the model is constructed and tested with more precision, a more accurate estimate of light levels can be achieved. Secondly, *comparisons* can be made between modifications to a design. Different sizes of window openings, for instance, can be compared to determine which provide the best results. One wall paint can be compared to another.

Thirdly, models can be used for *visual observation* and aesthetic analysis. It is here that architects may find the model an exceedingly effective tool. Clients can more readily perceive the designer's expectations when viewing a representative model. While model simulation is relatively simple and does not require a high degree of technical understanding, there are a number of points about model construction and use which should be understood.

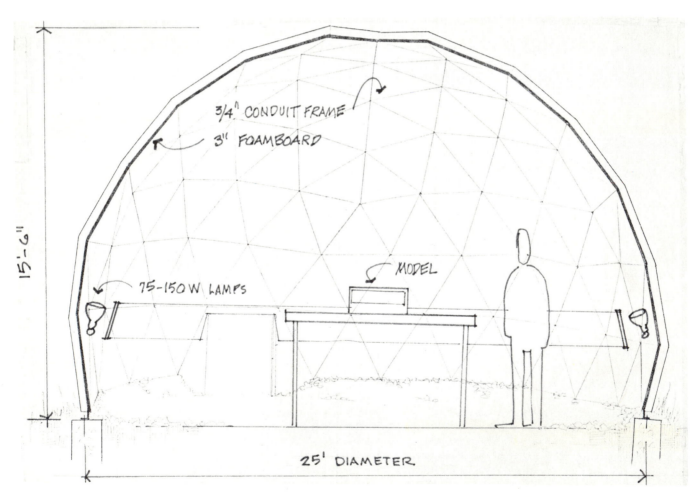

FIGURE 6-3. CROSS SECTION OF THE SIMULATED SKY AT VIRGINIA TECH.

## Building the Model

The model, of course, should duplicate the full-scale building design as closely as possible for accurate daylighting comparisons. However, one of the greatest advantages of model studies is the opportunity to get some quick answers with a minimum of cost, time, and effort. Thus, some judgment must be exercised in deciding what level of model "correctness" is to be achieved. Even crude models can provide some answers and are especially valuable for comparing single-element design alternatives. Generally, crude models can be used for preliminary studies and more sophisticated models for later refinements.

**Geometry.** The model must duplicate certain details of the geometry of the full-scale design, but often other details are not critical. Particularly significant is the size of openings through which light is to pass. The over-all size of the light openings should be maintained. Window frames, mullions, sills and jambs, skylight wells, louvers, and other such details must be duplicated fairly accurately in terms of those properties which block or reflect light. A mullion in the model, for instance, need not be shaped in the form of some complicated extruded aluminum piece, but can be a simple rectangle in cross section. The thickness of the walls of the model is irrelevant since their only function is to restrict the entry of unwanted light and to reflect light from its interior surface as would a full-scale wall. The depth and reflectivity of the window sill, however, is important because of its role in reflecting light into the room. Venetian blinds or other types of louvers can be duplicated at scale or at a scale other than that used for the rest of the model if the proportion of the louver width-to-opening is the same.

Most curved forms, such as round columns against the walls, are generally of minor importance in terms of form and can be duplicated in the model as simple, rectangular shapes.

In buildings with very large interior spaces, uninterrupted by floor-to-ceiling walls, the illumination simulation of a typical bay or section can be reasonably achieved by

FIGURE 6-4. Students conducting daylighting model tests in the simulated sky at Virginia Tech University.

FIGURE 6-5. University of Florida student Ron Isaacson preparing a sophisticated model of an actual room for model testing in the Virginia Tech University simulated sky.

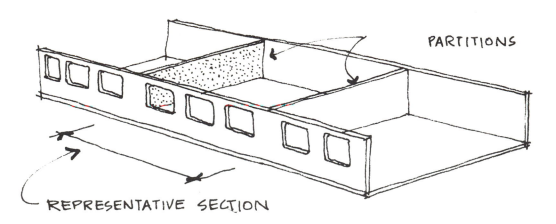

PARTITIONS

REPRESENTATIVE SECTION

FIGURE 6-6. PARTITIONS MADE OF MIRROR OR PAINTED WHITE CAN SIMULATE SECTIONS OF LARGE INTERIOR SPACES.

enclosing the typical space with opaque side walls painted white, or mirrors can be used. Thus, for this imaginary plane, light from the prime space that would otherwise be lost to adjacent areas will be reflected back, representing the light that would normally be received into the primary space from adjacent areas.

In spaces with daylight openings on more than one wall, where design alternatives are to be compared, it may be necessary to black out one opening in order to detect changes related to the other opening. This may be done by covering the secondary opening with an opaque material painted black to simulate the light from inside the model that would be absorbed or lost through the opening when it is in operation. Sometimes, with this process where conditions require it, one opening at a time can be tested and the results added to get a total illumination level from both openings.

**Materials.** Materials of the model are important only in terms of their transparency or opacity (light transmitted or blocked),

their reflectance (light reflected or absorbed), and their texture (glossy or diffusing). If the materials have a fine texture, such as smooth concrete, fabric, gypsum board, or unpainted plywood, the texture can be duplicated sufficiently with paint on plywood or cardboard. More significant (or rough) textures, such as exposed-pebble concrete, may be sufficiently simulated with sandpaper or some other rough material. Color is of no significance since the instruments do not differentiate between colors, so gray paints or dark and light paper can be used to simulate colored surfaces provided a reflectometer is available for measuring and matching the paint's reflectance properties. (For a method of approximating reflectances with a light meter, see Figure 6-14). Color reproduction is necessary for visual observation, and the model builder is always on firm ground when using the exact paints for the model that are intended for the full-scale building.

Walls can be built of plywood, foamboard, or cardboard and painted appropriately. Foamboards are often not completely opaque and must be painted or covered with foil or some other opaque material to prevent the penetration of unwanted light. Window frames and mullions can be made of balsa wood or, often, of fine strips of opaque paper or cardboard glued onto the glass or acetate window glazing. Window glass can be simulated in the model with real glass provided it is not more than about 1/8-inch thick. Glass can also be simulated with thin sheets of acetate if the transmission factor is similar. Glass transmittance varies with the angle of the incident light, but in relatively simple openings, in comparative model studies, glass may be altogether deleted from the model and a multiplication factor applied to the measured illumination levels to compensate for the light reflection and absorption of the glass. For simulation of glass with a transmission of 85 percent, for instance, the illumination levels in the model without glass may be reduced by a factor of .15. While the glass does not, in fact, reduce illumination uniformly throughout the interior space, the distribution effect is relatively minor, except when direct sun strikes the windows. In this case, actual glass or acetate should be used in the model to account for specular reflection off the glass. Special conditions relating to the sun are discussed later in this chapter. Again, the model builder is safe in using the actual materials where possible.

A simple, but reasonably accurate, method for determining the transmission of transparent or translucent materials is shown in Figure 6–7. A light cell is placed in the box opposite a small (about 2 inches square) opening with some type of constant, diffuse source light just outside the box (about 10 to 12 inches). With the light burning, the illumination on the light cell is recorded. The material to be tested is then placed over the opening in the box and the illumination on the cell recorded again. The material transmission can be calculated by dividing the first measurement (simple box) with the second (material to be tested in place). Example: 144/180 × 100 = 80 percent transmission.

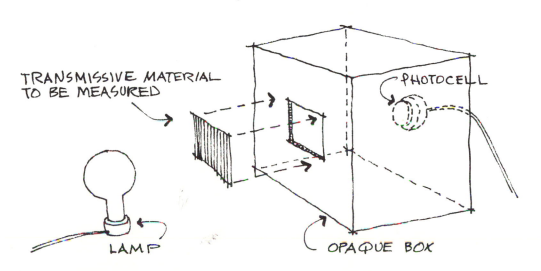

TRANSMISSIVE MATERIAL TO BE MEASURED

PHOTOCELL

LAMP

OPAQUE BOX

FIGURE 6-7. A SIMPLE TECHNIQUE FOR DETERMINING THE APPROXIMATE LIGHT TRANSMISSION OF A MATERIAL.

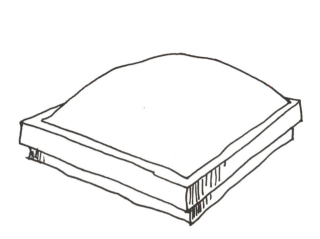
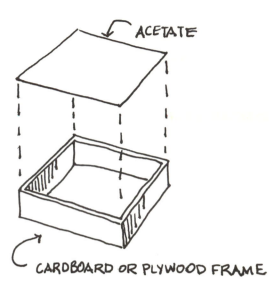

ACETATE

CARDBOARD OR PLYWOOD FRAME

# FIGURE 6-8. A FULL-SCALE PLASTIC-DOME SKYLIGHT AND SCALE MODEL.

Plastic-dome skylights may be simulated with a flat or pyramid-shaped covering of translucent (or transparent) material (e.g., acetate, tracing paper, glass) that approximates the transmission and diffusing properties of the plastic-dome material. Since this will not take into account the curvature, height, and stretched nature of the plastic-dome material, there is some error in the accuracy of the results, but the significance of this error is small, except when dealing with low sun angles, with which the error will be greater. Still, considering the difficulty of forming model skylights to closely approximate full-scale, vacuum-formed domed skylights, the flat or pyramid-shaped material will usually constitute the most feasible approach.

Other types of skylights, such as those that employ glass pitched to a peak, can be treated in a straightforward manner with glass or acetate and duplication of details to the degree possible.

**Scale.** Models for studying daylight can be constructed at any convenient scale. Generally, it is difficult to reproduce details accurately in very small models, and the relative size of the illumination meter-probe to be used may cause excessive absorption and reflection when inserted into a small model. A scale of 3/4" = 1'0" produces a convenient size model for studying a room. A model of a typical classroom at this scale will measure about 23 inches square by 8 inches in height. However, this scale may be too large to handle conveniently if several rooms or adjacent parts of the building must be included in the study. A scale of 1/2 inch or 3/8 inch may be used if care is exercised in construction. Models at lesser scales are difficult to build and to measure using available light cells. Such small-scale models are not recommended for daylighting studies.

**Test Conditions.** It is important to take into consideration the method by which the light-measuring instruments will be inserted into the model and situated at particular predetermined locations for the tests. Generally, there should be a section of the model removable for access. This may be a wall or a roof that is hinged so that the observer can insert the light cell or change its location during the test. There should be a hole located conveniently in one of the exterior walls for the wire extending from the photocell inside the model to the light-level meter which will be located outside the model. Care should be exercised so that unwanted light will not penetrate the cracks around any removable or hinged section. Opaque tape over the crack when the panel is in place is often a convenient solution to this problem. Also, care should be exercised to assure that stray light does not penetrate model materials used for walls and roofs.

Suggested points for measurement in rectangular rooms are shown in Figure 6-11. Of course, designers may choose whatever points for measurement they feel will be significant for the particular conditions of the building design.

It is often convenient to provide some type of mechanical stop for positioning the light cell inside the model to assure proper location and to allow comparative measurements to be made at identical points in the model. Slight variations in locating the photocell in the model may significantly affect the illumination measurement. Once the testing is begun, time may be otherwise lost in trying to position the photocell correctly in the confined space of the model. Positioning of the photocell can be simplified with a nail driven into the floor of the model on which the photocell can be placed, or with several nails to position the cell as it is pushed into place. A thin, flat piece of cardboard cut to fit around the cell, glued to the floor, and painted to match the floor, can also be used.

## Instrumentation

There are a variety of photometers (light meters) and photocells available which are suitable for model studies. The discussion of instruments here will be limited to those which, in the opinion of the author, are suitable, sufficiently accurate, and in a reasonable price category for use in daylighting studies by architects' and engineers' offices.

Most modern illumination photometers make use of a selenium photovoltaic cell. This cell has a treated metallic plate which,

FIGURE 6-9. W.C. Lam, lighting consultant, with students and a model of the proposed TVA building design. The preliminary design for this building is illustrated in Figures 4–50 and 4–51.

FIGURE 6-10. Tom Lemons, TLA-Lighting Consultants, Inc., with model and group of students.

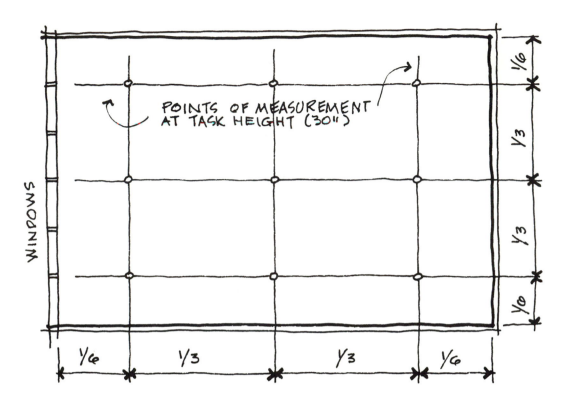

FIGURE 6-11. SUGGESTED LOCATIONS FOR MEASUREMENT OF **DAYLIGHT** IN MODELS.

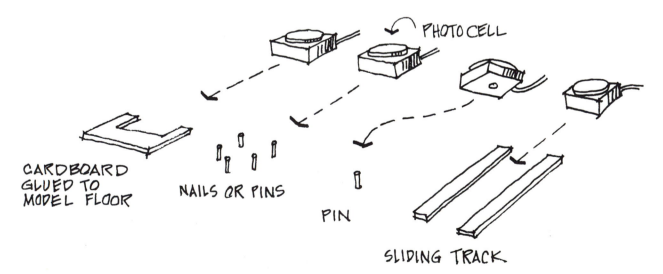

FIGURE 6-12. TECHNIQUES FOR POSITIONING PHOTO CELL IN MODEL.

when exposed to light, generates a small electromagnetic current. The current is conducted to a sensitive instrument (the "light meter") which measures this current and translates it into footcandles (or into lux, which is the worldwide standard unit of illumination). Another type of light cell is the photoemissive cell. This unit includes a circuit between the light cell and the foot-candle indicator that receives current from a battery. (Battery-powered photometers, however, may use either of these types of cells.) Light striking the cell causes its relationship to the current to change, thereby changing the meter reading in footcandles. Almost all photometers use one of these two systems. However, there are several details regarding their performance characteristics which should be considered.

Photocells are not all identical and their current output is not always directly proportional to the illumination incident upon the surface of the cell. For this reason, cells must be calibrated at the factory or in the laboratory so that the photometer reading indicates the true illumination at all levels. Thus, the cell from one photometer cannot usually be used with another, although some manufacturers do offer equipment which is interchangeable within the line of their own products.

Also, photocells respond to the total energy spectrum differently than does the human eye, whose response is to the "visible" portion of the spectrum. The photocell measures other areas of the energy spectrum as well. For comparative studies of models, this discrepancy is not significant. The relative merits of two design schemes under comparison are still valid. However, for absolute measurements (actual illumination levels) the photocell must be adapted with a color corrector (often referred to as a "Viscor Filter"). Since the addition of the *color correction device* seldom significantly alters the price, it is recommended in any new purchase.

Photocells are also subject to the "cosine law of illumination." That is, they do not record as accurately light striking the cell from a low angle as from a high or more direct angle. Thus, photocells produce incorrect measurements when used for general lighting studies. Most manufacturers of

FIGURE 6-13. Typical cosine-corrected photo-electric light cell for measuring illumination levels.

photometers can provide a cosine correction device for their photocells. It is absolutely *necessary* that photometers for lighting studies come equipped with a *cosine correction device.*

Early model photometers used some type of galvanometer for measuring the current output of the photovoltaic cell. These galvanometers were extremely sensitive to shock and were frequently knocked out of calibration by rough handling. Some architects and engineers are still using this type of instrument. More recent photometers are a little more rugged, and the best of the new equipment is transistorized and uses digital liquid crystal display units. Before purchasing a new photometer, read the manufacturer's specifications with regard to ruggedness.[9]

Other characteristics to consider include the frequency of need for calibration and the range of measurable illumination levels. Good equipment does not need recali-

FIGURE 6-14. MAKING APPROXIMATE LUMINANCE MEASUREMENTS WITH A HAND-HELD LIGHT METER.

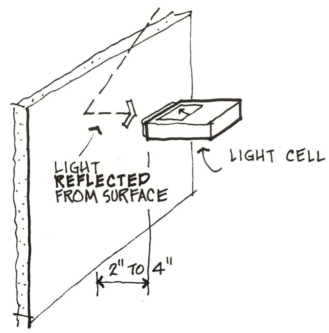

LIGHT CELL

LIGHT REFLECTED FROM SURFACE

2" TO 4"

LUMINANCE (OR BRIGHTNESS) IS MEASURED IN FOOTLAMBERTS. PLACE METER CLOSE TO SURFACE AND SLOWLY MOVE AWAY UNTIL READING STABILIZES.

$$\text{LUMINANCE (FT. LAMBERTS)} = \text{METER READING (FT.C.)} \times 1.25$$

bration more often than about once every two years with normal use. For daylighting studies, the photometer should provide a range of measurement from 1 to 12,000 footcandles. Usually, this range of response will require the user to switch ranges as necessary and mentally multiply the output by some correction factor (e.g., ×1, ×10, ×100). However, it is possible to adapt most photometers which do not have this range so that they will measure high illumination levels by covering the cell with a cap which transmits a percentage of the incident light. For instance, if the maximum range of the scale is 1000 footcandles and you wish to measure a light level of 2000

# FIGURE 6-15. MAKING APPROXIMATE REFLECTANCE MEASUREMENTS WITH A HAND-HELD LIGHT METER.

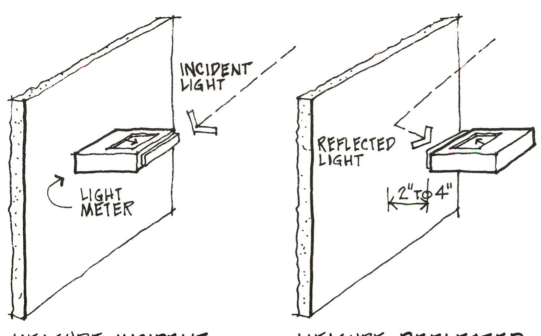

MEASURE **INCIDENT** LIGHT ON SURFACE....    MEASURE **REFLECTED** LIGHT FROM SURFACE....

$$\text{REFLECTANCE OF SURFACE} = \frac{\text{REFLECTED}}{\text{INCIDENT}} = \%$$

**OR,** IF YOU HAVE A SAMPLE OF **KNOWN** REFLECTANCE....

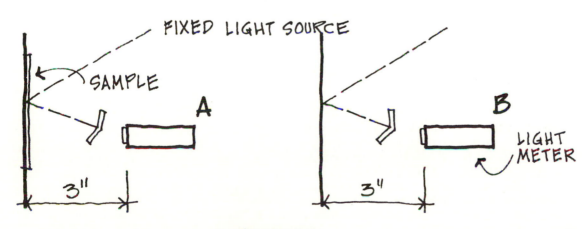

$$\text{REFLECTANCE} = \frac{\text{B READING}}{\text{A READING}} \times \text{SAMPLE REFLECTANCE} = \%$$

footcandles, the cell can be covered with a cap allowing 50 percent of the light to penetrate. The indicator on the scale will then read 500 footcandles and can be multiplied by two to get the correct answer of 1000. A cap for this purpose can be made by drilling holes that amount to 50 percent of the total cell area and calibrated using a device such as that described in Figure 6-8.

Photometers which have the photocell built into the display meter case (such as those normally used for photography) are not suitable for model studies since the light-level indicator requires placement inside the model and it usually can't be seen from outside the model without influencing or blocking the incident light. However, those meters which read in footcandles can be helpful for general measurements around the office.

**Available Light Meters.** Choosing the right photometer will depend upon intended use (e.g., model studies, full-scale measurements), the expertise of the purchaser and user, funds available, range of options needed, accuracy required, and so on. A survey of photometer manufacturers resulted in fewer responses than expected, and only in England is a unit made especially for model studies. The units briefly described here appear suitable for model studies as well as general lighting measurements. While some of the manufacturer's more critical performance criteria are listed here, no attempt is otherwise made to evaluate quality in the instruments. Costs shown are based on information received for 1979–80, but may vary considerably with passing time.

While the price of a good photometer may seem excessive, remember that the unit itself represents only a minor portion of the costs that may be devoted to a project —personnel becoming familiar with the model-study process, model supplies and construction, and the time and energy contribution for meaningful studies. An appropriate, well-made photometer may save expense in the long run, and one significant model-study project may save thousands of dollars if it prevents a design error, thus offsetting the cost of the instrument.

**Survey of Photometer Manufacturers***

**Tektronix, Inc.**
P.O. Box 500
Beaverton, Oregon 97007
(503) 644-0161

**The J16 Digital Photometer/Radiometer** (basic readout unit): LED Digital display; 2.4 × 4.6 × 8 in.; 3.3 lb; Rechargeable nickel-cadmium batteries and battery charger; Optional A/C power supply; Price $850.

**J6511 Illuminance Probe** (for measuring illumination in footcandles): 0.001 to 1999 fc (to 199,900 fc on request); Cosine and color corrected; 2.5 × 2.5 × 1 in.; 12- to 25-ft probe cable; Price $420.

**J6503 8 Degree Luminance Probe** (for measuring luminance or "brightness" in footlamberts): 0.1 to 199,900 fL; 2 × 1.5 × 8 in. (clips to photometer); 8 degree = 1.7 in./ft of distance from probe to target; Price $400.

FIGURE 6-16.
TEKTRONIX J16
PHOTOMETER

*All prices quoted are taken from supplier's 1979 literature and may or may not include tax, shipping, etc.

**Gossen Division**
**Berkey Marketing Companies**
25–20 Brooklyn-Queens Expwy. West
Woodside, New York 11377
(212) 932-4040

**Panlux Electronic Footcandle Meter:**
0.05 to 12,000 fc; 4.25 × 3 × 1.5 in. (probe
6⅜ in.); 4.5 oz; Battery operated; Cosine
corrected; 3-ft probe cord; Price $176 (for
10-ft cord, add $25).

**International Light, Inc.**
Dexter Industrial Green
Newburyport, Massachusetts 01950
(617) 465-5923

**IL410 Photometer** (for measuring footcandles): 0.3 to 1000 fc; 4.2 × 3.5 × 23.1 in.;
2.5 lb; Cosine and color corrected; 7-ft
probe cable; Battery operated; Price $419.

**SC110/CM219 Optional Illuminance
Probe:** 0.3 to 10,000 fc; Price $177.

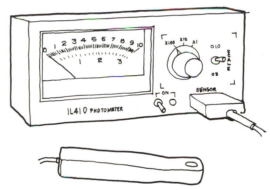

FIGURE 6-18.
INTERNATIONAL LIGHT
IL410 PHOTOMETER

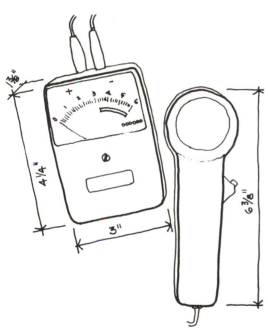

FIGURE 6-17. PANLUX
ELECTRONIC
FOOTCANDLE METER

**Simpson Electric Company**
853 Dundee Avenue
Elgin, Illinois 60120
(312) 697-2260

**Simpson Illumination Level Meter** (for measuring footcandles): 0 to 1500 fc; 0 to 50,000 fc with optional filter; 1.8-in. cell diameter; 3.2 × 4.6 × 1.6 in.; less than 1 lb; Cosine and color corrected; Luminance x2 tube for luminance or "brightness" measurements—0 to 10,000 fL; Price $199, complete with carrying case.

**Salford Electrical Instruments Ltd.**
Peel Works
Barton Lane, Eccles
Manchester M30 0HL
England

**Minilux 2 Portable Photoelectric Photometer** (for measuring illumination in lux: 10 lux = approx. 1 fc): 215 × 135 × 95 mm; 440 g; 0.25 to 10,000 lux; Cosine and color corrected; Battery powered; 2-m cord; Price £159.

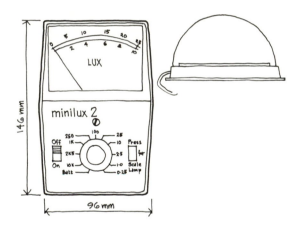

FIGURE 6-19.
SIMPSON MODEL 408
ILLUMINATION LEVEL
METER

FIGURE 6-20.
MINILUX 2 PORTABLE
PHOTOELECTRIC
PHOTOMETER

**Megatron Ltd.**
165 Marlborough Road
Hornsey Road
London N19 4NE
England

**Megatron Architectural Model Luxmeter** (for measuring illumination in lux): Utilizes 12 type M photocells through selective switching; 0 to 10,000 lux (1000 fc); Cosine and color corrected; Cell diameter 45 mm, other sizes available; 10-ft cables; Price £560.

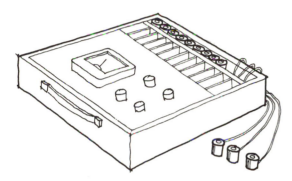

FIGURE 6-21.
MEGATRON
ARCHITECTURAL
MODEL LUXMETER

## Sky Conditions

The type of sky conditions which will exist at the project location must be carefully studied (see Chapter 5) and a translation made between those real sky conditions and the type of sky or skies which can most appropriately be used for model studies. For a project in Arizona where the percent of possible sunshine is high and the percent of possible cloud cover low, model studies will probably be most useful if performed under a clear sky with sunshine. For a project in an area where there is little sunshine and lots of cloud cover, the model studies would probably best be done under an overcast sky. Sometimes it will be desirable to conduct model studies under both sky conditions to be sure the design performs satisfactorily under all conditions.

Once the designer has determined the type or types of sky conditions which are significant, there remains only the problem of the sky cooperating to produce the conditions desired and an understanding of how each type of sky must be treated during the testing process.

The illumination produced by the sky tends to change almost constantly and, usually, more quickly than is realized. A period of reasonable stability is highly desirable, in fact necessary, for model daylighting tests, particularly when two or more variations of the model are to be tested for comparison. Interior illumination values will not be very meaningful if the sky changes significantly between two test runs. The best opportunity for stable sky conditions exists with a simulated sky or a dense, overcast sky.

Simulated skies have the advantage of remaining essentially constant during model tests so that comparisons may be easily made. Each type of simulated sky, however, will have its own peculiar characteristics, and there must be an understanding of what these characteristics are and how they will affect comparisons of models to full-scale conditions.

Generally, artificial skies attempt to simulate the dense, overcast sky with either a uniform luminance distribution or a distribution ratio of about 3:1, apex to zenith. No attempt is usually made to include direct sunshine in these simulated skies.

The dense, overcast sky is the most uniform type of sky condition and generally tends to change more slowly than other types of skies. For model tests, a cloud cover of 100 percent is most desirable. Because of the uniformity of that part of the overcast sky which transmits light directly into the model, certain mathematical relationships of interior to exterior illumination exist and can greatly simplify certain types of model comparisons. These conditions will be more fully explained under the section on model testing.

The clear sky and sun produce a total level of illumination which varies constantly but slowly throughout the day. Most daylighting studies are based on the presumption that no direct sunlight will penetrate the building fenestration. The presence of direct sun on the selected measuring points within the building model may cause difficulties in making quantitative measurements if the illumination meter in use is not capable of measuring high intensity levels.

However, if the proper instruments are available, there is no reason why the clear sky with sun cannot be used for daylighting model tests. The location of the sun in the sky will be critical since the intensity produced on the building will vary as the sun moves; so the appropriate time of day for measurements must be determined and the model tested as close to this period as possible.

The partly cloudy sky usually includes widely varying luminances from one area of the sky to another and tends to change quite rapidly. In addition, the partly cloudy sky may include periods when direct sun will reach the test area. As a result, intensity levels of daylight in a model will tend to change much too rapidly for comparison of one measurement to the other, and establishing a base reading of exterior conditions will also be difficult. Because of these circumstances, model tests under a partly cloudy sky are unsuitable and, therefore, not recommended.

## Model Testing

The testing of a model can be relatively simple once the process is fully understood and the proper testing equipment is at hand. For the person conducting his first tests, a trial run is heartily recommended. For the trial run, sky conditions, location, surrounding obstructions, and so forth, are of no great consequence because the results are not to be used. The trial run simply provides an opportunity to become familiar with the process, to eliminate any awkward movements, and to make sure that instruments and model are in working order.

**Selecting an Outdoor Location.** An outdoor location for the final model tests should be selected which will provide approximately the same sky and ground conditions that will exist for the proposed full-scale building. The condition of the ground is particularly important since a high percentage of the light entering the model (or building) may be reflected from the ground.[10] The use of dark green grass compared to a concrete street in front of a window can make a significant difference in interior illumination levels and distribution.

The model should be properly oriented with respect to the sun (and compass), although if the tests are for comparison of two schemes, orientation may not be important. Two good locations for model tests are a large open field such as a park or the flat roof of a local building where there are no obstructions to the windows or skylights.

**Setting up the Model.** The model should be placed on the ground or on some type of support, such as a table, and it should be adjusted to the proper horizontal level. A "tilted" model can result in the model "visualizing" an inappropriate proportion of sky and ground and thus produce incorrect light levels. Also, if several tests are to be run on the model on different occasions with different sky conditions, a level position will be the easiest to maintain from one occasion to the next. A waist-high table is a convenient support from which to work, as it can save a lot of stooping and squatting; if the appropriate ground condition is not available, a sheet of cardboard or paper painted to simulate the proper ground conditions can be placed on the table next to the model window. Ground conditions beyond about 40 feet from a first-floor window are not significant in reflecting light into the building. The effectiveness of the ground in reflecting light extends out an additional 40 feet for each 10 feet the room is above the ground level.

**Reference Measurements.** It is absolutely necessary that certain reference illumination measurements of the exterior sky conditions be made at the beginning, during, and at the end of model daylight tests. These measurements provide a basis on which to compare various tests and to give an indication of the changing conditions of the sky. If, for instance, two design schemes are to be compared, and during the tests, which might take as much as 30 minutes or more, the sky conditions change significantly (as much as about 15 percent), a comparison of the resulting interior illumination levels will not be meaningful. But if the exterior sky conditions are being monitored, a change in sky conditions will be quickly detected. In this event, the tests can be delayed until the sky luminance becomes more stable.

If the tests are being conducted under a dense, overcast sky, knowledge of the exterior sky condition allows for some mathematical manipulations. A test on a model with a window in only one wall might be conducted when the illumination from the sky is 1500 footcandles, and the second test when the illumination from the sky is 2000 footcandles. The interior illumination levels under the two conditions can still be compared by multiplying, for instance, the results of the first test by a factor of 2000/1500, which would then put the results of both tests on the basis of an exterior sky condition of 2000 footcandles. In fact, both of these test results can be mathematically converted to any exterior sky illumination level via the same process. This mathematical process can be applied only to a model with windows in a single wall and should not be applied to partly cloudy or clear sky conditions, except in certain cases and by someone experienced and knowledgeable.

For the scientist, there are several types of reference measurements of the exterior sky that are used. However, for the types of tests to be conducted outdoor by archi-

FIGURE 6-22.   Typical model on location.

tects and others, for whom testing is not an occupation, there are two sufficient measurements to consider. They are designated as follows:

$Ev =$ illumination from the sky on the plane of the vertical fenestration or window wall and parallel to the wall (a few inches immediately outside the window, but beyond any obstructing parts of the building such as overhangs, louvers, etc.)

This measurement is made by placing the photocell on the center of the vertical window wall of the model (if there are not protruding building parts to restrict the light reaching the cell), or it can be placed on a vertical mount located a few inches away from this point on the wall and parallel to it. The cell can be attached to the wall with tape, but since the cell will have to be

removed for other measurements, a more secure but flexible mounting is desirable—perhaps a heavy block of wood or fabricated stand which can be removed after the measurement is made. If two or more photocells are being used, the reference cell can be placed above the window or overhang and left in place.

This measurement provides an indication of the total light from the sky, plus that light reflected from the ground and surrounding objects, which is "available" to pass into the window opening of the model. This technique considers the ground surface as part of the total light source, which is appropriate for a reference reading if the ground surface is not to be changed from one test to another. If the ground surface is to be altered in any way, the $Ev$ reference measurement should include only the light from the sky. This is accomplished by attaching a horizontal shield to the light cell which will admit light from the sky only.

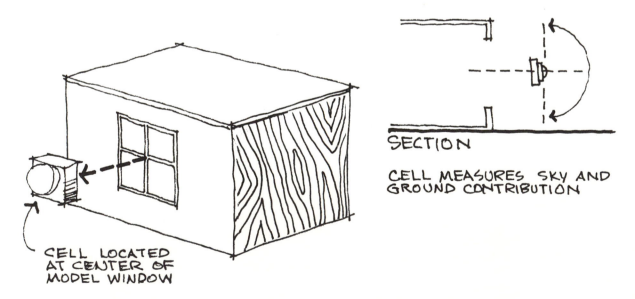

CELL LOCATED AT CENTER OF MODEL WINDOW

SECTION

CELL MEASURES SKY AND GROUND CONTRIBUTION

FIGURE 6-23. MEASUREMENT OF THE ILLUMINATION ON THE VERTICAL ($E_v$) INCLUDING LIGHT FROM GROUND AND SKY.

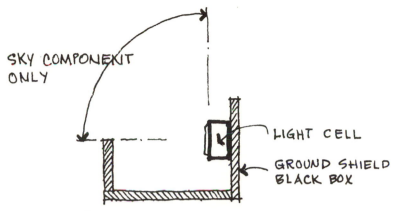

SKY COMPONENT ONLY

LIGHT CELL

GROUND SHIELD BLACK BOX

CROSS SECTION OF CELL AND GROUND SHIELD

## FIGURE 6-24. THE $E_v$ MEASUREMENT LIMITED TO THE SKY CONTRIBUTION.

This illumination may be as low as two or three hundred footcandles and as high as three or four thousand (without direct sun). This measurement must be made for each window wall if there is more than one (e.g., one wall south-facing and another east-facing).

$Eh$ = total hemispheric illumination on the unobstructed plane of the ground from both the sun and sky (any distance from the ground up to several hundred feet will suffice; usually the roof of the model is an appropriate place).

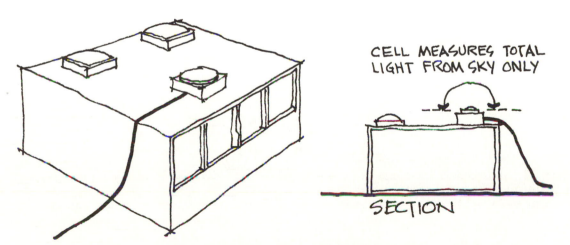

CELL MEASURES TOTAL LIGHT FROM SKY ONLY

SECTION

## FIGURE 6-25. MEASUREMENT OF THE SKY ILLUMINATION ON THE HORIZONTAL ($E_H$).

This measurement is necessary only when the model has horizontal openings (e.g., skylights), although it can be used with window lighting as a check on changing sky conditions if taken at intervals during a test. The measurement is made by placing the light cell on a flat surface, such as the model roof or tripod stand, where light from the sky will not be obstructed. This measurement provides an indication of the total light from the sky (and sun) that is "available" to pass into a horizontal opening such as a skylight. For a vertical clerestory window on the roof, the base reading would be $Ev$, as for a vertical window wall. The $Eh$ measurement, if made on a clear day will, of course, include direct sunlight. In this case, the light meter to be used must be capable of measuring up to about 12,000 footcandles.

**Testing A Model.** A step-by-step description of the testing of a model of a typical schoolroom will help to clarify the process.

The model is placed on a table in an open field away from any nearby obstructions. Under a dense, overcast sky, the model is oriented in the same direction as the full-scale classroom when constructed. A strip of cardboard painted with light gray paint is placed on the table next to the window to simulate the concrete sidewalk. A scale tree constructed of actual branches of a shrub is placed next to the model.

The photocell is mounted on a block of wood and placed on the table just at the edge of the overhang to provide a reference measurement of the light from the sky and ground reaching the window wall ($Ev$). The photometer measures 652 footcandles and seems to be holding steady. After the $Ev$ measurement has been made, the photocell and support are removed.

Next, the side wall of the model is opened and the photocell inserted into the model. A cardboard support is used under the photocell so that its upper surface is at a height of 30 inches, about that of a desk. The cell is guided into position No. 1 by the thin piece of notched cardboard glued to the floor. The side wall is reattached to the model, the wire from the photocell is passed through the precut notch to the photometer located on the table top behind the model. All cracks are checked to ensure that no extraneous light penetrates the model. A check is made to ensure that nothing blocks the light reaching the model windows (e.g., people, hands, autos).

The photometer illumination reading at position No. 1 is recorded. The model is reopened and the photocell moved to position No. 2. After all interior measurements have been made in similar fashion, the photocell is attached once again to the wood-block stand, and the exterior sky condition ($Ev$) measured again. The exterior illumination level now reads 820 footcandles. The sky has changed too rapidly for results of the model tests to be meaningful. The entire test must be rerun until such time as the before and after $Ev$ measurements are similar (within about 5 percent).

**Observing and Photographing a Model**
Qualitative evaluation of daylighting design alternatives can also be made by observing models. Subjective impressions are sometimes much more meaningful to the designer than footcandle levels and indicate brightnesses impossible to measure in models without sophisticated instruments. The model must be designed with an operable panel in the floor of the model or in a wall through which observations or photographs can be taken. If the model is large enough, the observer can insert his whole head into the model interior.

Naturally, any object inside the model will tend to interfere to some degree with the distribution of daylight and may introduce stray light, which will distort the real luminous condition. A reasonable amount of caution can overcome these limitations.

Best results are achieved when the model is constructed with a realistic interior—paints, furniture, carpets, scale human model, etc.—and with a realistic view to the outside (landscaping, nearby buildings, etc.). Clients may inspect the model at its site or colored slides can be made of the inside of the model with different sky conditions—clear sky with sun or overcast sky—and then shown to the client at a convenient time and place. Such models are very helpful to clients and building users in visu-

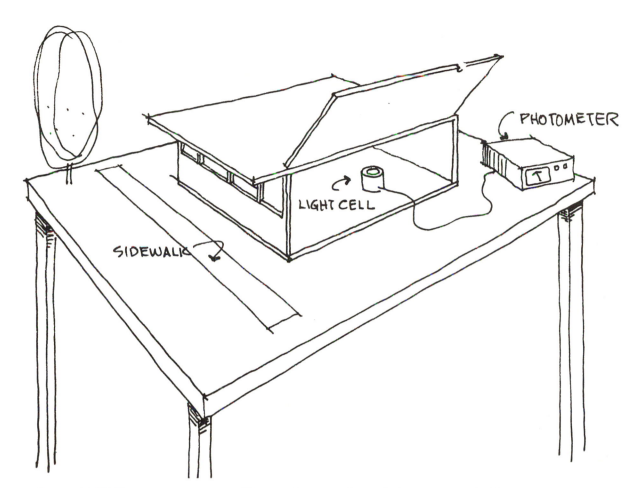

PHOTOMETER

LIGHT CELL

SIDEWALK

# FIGURE 6-26. THE MODEL IS OPENED AND THE LIGHT CELL POSITIONED.

alizing realistic conditions which usually cannot be described effectively to them by way of numbers—footcandles and footlamberts.

## Guidelines for Photography

1. FILM—A number of appropriate films are available. Those with high-speed capability are especially useful in model work as they allow the use of higher f-stops to improve depth of field. (Specify film type balanced for daylight.) **Ektachrome 400** (ASA 400) is especially good for slides although more expensive than the slower films. **Kodachrome 64** (ASA 64) is a fine-grain slide film, less expensive and more readily available. It is particularly suitable when the camera can be set on a tripod and longer-term exposures used (.5 to 1.5 seconds). **Kodacolor 400** (ASA 400) is a good, fast film for color prints. **Panatomic-X** (ASA 32) is an exceptionally fine-grain film for black-and-white prints and enlargements. Because of its relative slowness, mounting the camera on a tripod is usually necessary.

FIGURE 6-27. Photograph of the interior of a model.

2. CAMERA—Any adjustable camera will do, but because of the small spaces in model work, a single-lens reflex (SLR) is particularly useful as the through-the-lens viewfinder allows the photographer to see exactly what the film will record.

3. LENS—A wide-angle lens is recommended (e.g., 24, 28, or 35 mm), since it will provide a more realistic (wide-field) image and greater depth of field.

4. FOCUS—Allow as much depth of field as possible by using fast film, higher f-stops, and longer exposures (when possible). Use a tripod and cable shutter release.

5. POSITION—Position camera to simulate normal eye-level position and try to maintain a level camera to avoid vertical line distortions in the finished photo. Keep the camera lens inside the model or at the edge of the wall line so that the finished slide shows only the inside of the model.

6. EXPOSURE—Judging proper exposure times when the meter readings include light from the bright exterior (through windows) as well as dimmer interior areas is difficult. A compromise between highest and lowest readings is usually necessary. A safe bet is to take shots with several different exposures to be sure one is satisfactory.

NOTE: The human eye is many times more sensitive to light than films and has a much broader latitude of sensitivity to light and dark areas at the same instant. Thus, under even the best of circumstances, photographs will not truly represent the real lighting environment. Some photographers will use supplementary electric light with model studies to make the finished photo appear as the real space would. Unless this process is meticulously done, it may give the appearance of artificiality.

### An Example Study with Models— The Shell Oil Building

In March 1978, Caudill Rowlett Scott (CRS), architects/planners/engineers of Houston, Texas, considered the use of extensive daylighting in the design for the new Shell Oil Company Woodcreek Exploration and Production Office Building Complex now being built in Houston. The possibility of using daylight extensively to achieve quality lighting and to conserve energy costs seemed very real. The project designers, Charles Lawrence and Rey de la Reza, developed a design concept with a series of triangular buildings four to six stories in height around a central atrium area covered by skylights.

The complex was to house a large number of Shell's scientific personnel concerned with such things as geological surveys for the exploration of oil. To stimulate maximum productivity from these highly creative and knowledgeable individuals, Shell prescribed that the space should be a pleasant working environment and that the majority of the personnel be provided with private offices with views. It was this aspect of the building program which led CRS designers to the long, narrow building section which consisted of individual offices on both sides of a central corridor. The elongated plan was then folded into a triangular floor plan for compactness to improve efficiency of property use and person-to-person communications, and to allow daylight into each office.

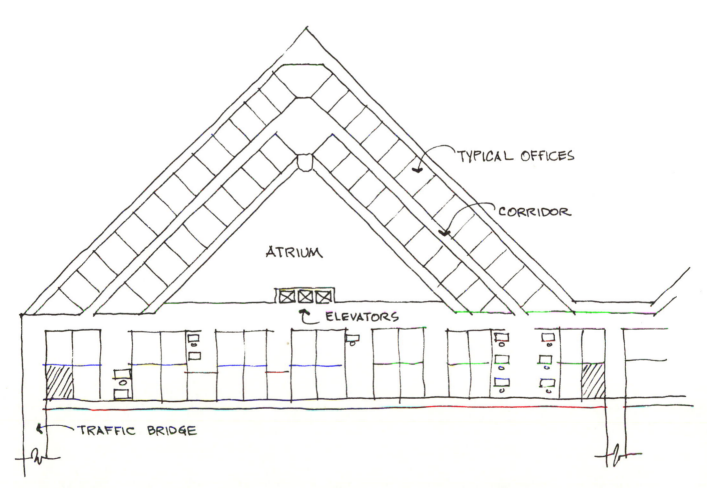

FIGURE 6-28. PLAN VIEW OF THE PRELIMINARY DESIGN FOR ONE UNIT OF THE SHELL OIL COMPLEX.

The use of daylight in those offices on the exterior of the complex (i.e., facing toward the woods) was considered a relatively straightforward daylighting problem. Houston has a sufficient number of clear and partly cloudy days with high illumination levels so that CRS was sure that daylight would provide these offices with sufficient light. The question was whether it would be possible to have sufficient daylight penetrating those offices that face the skylight-covered atrium. To test the plan's feasibility, CRS commissioned a "quick and dirty" model study.

**Model Study No. 1.** For the study, a 1/8" = 1'0" scale model of the triangular atrium area was constructed (see Figure 6-29), using 1/4-inch thick plywood painted with stripes of various gray paints to simulate the absorptive and reflective wall surfaces of the five-story atrium. On the ground floor of the model, along one side of the atrium, a row of office spaces was constructed. No actual glass was used in the model windows and, of course, refinement of details in the offices was not feasible at this small scale. The atrium skylight, covered with a sheet of diffusing acetate, had a transmission factor of 80 percent.

The model was tested in Blacksburg, Virginia, where the weather conditions are not exactly identical to Houston, but sufficiently close. Because of the varying nature of the skies, the location for such tests is not particularly critical. The illumination on the ground in Blacksburg on a clear day measured over 10,000 footcandles, and in

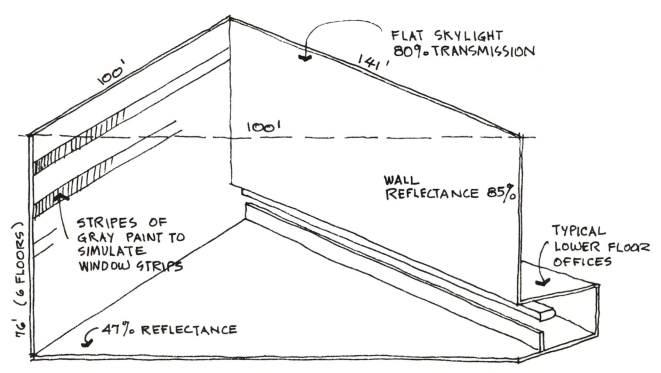

FIGURE 6-29. SCHEMATIC DRAWING OF THE SCALE MODEL OF THE ATRIUM AND TYPICAL OFFICE AREA OF THE PRELIMINARY SHELL OIL BUILDING DESIGN.

Houston slightly less than 10,000 (Houston frequently has substantial moisture haze in the air), so the difference was not great. These preliminary model tests were conducted under both an overcast sky and a clear sky, with the results shown in Figure 6-30. With the minimum conditions of the overcast sky producing an illumination level on the ground (*Eh*) of 3000 footcandles, the tests showed 59 to 72 footcandles at task level inside the office areas, which is well within the range of acceptable light levels for most office tasks.

Recognizing that the model simulation included some gross approximations, such as the 100 percent coverage of the atrium skylight with light-transmitting material (i.e., no beams, trusses, etc., for this "quick-and-dirty" model), it was, nevertheless, concluded that daylighting the interior of-

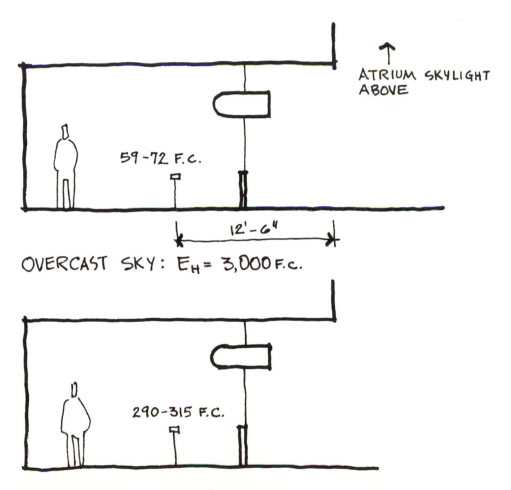

ATRIUM SKYLIGHT ABOVE

59 - 72 F.C.

12' - 6"

OVERCAST SKY: $E_H$ = 3,000 F.C.

290 - 315 F.C.

CLEAR SKY: $E_H$ = 10,250 F.C.

FIGURE 6-30. RESULTS OF DAYLIGHTING TESTS ON MODEL NO. 1 UNDER AN OVERCAST SKY.

fices was feasible. A further study by CRS engineers with regard to heat gain through the atrium skylight suggested that the skylight size should be kept to a minimum, but that the heat load could be handled without excessive mechanical equipment and that the savings in electric lighting costs was a compensating factor. The architects, therefore, proceeded to develop and refine this preliminary design.

Of course, daylighting was not the only design parameter to be considered. Structural, mechanical, and electrical systems had to be developed, balancing the relative economics and other merits of a variety of possibilities against a tight budget. An indirect electric lighting scheme was developed which would supplement the daylight as needed or replace it during night working hours. The design scheme which evolved gave every indication of achieving the program objectives with minimum costs—both initial and long-range.

Figure 6-31 shows the structural system and typical office configuration with daylight controls which were developed. With the major geometry and principal details of the design now established, a second daylighting model study was indicated to determine if this refined design would still provide sufficient daylighting.

**Model Study No. 2.**   For this second test, another model of the atrium was constructed, this time at a scale of $\frac{1}{2}" = 1'0"$, with a height of five stories. This model was much more complex than the first and incorporated many architectural details, including the structural framing system (outside the window walls) and details of the strip-skylights.

The atrium wall surfaces were again painted with gray paints to simulate windows and wall reflectances. Rather than build into the model all of the atrium-facing offices, a single office model was con-

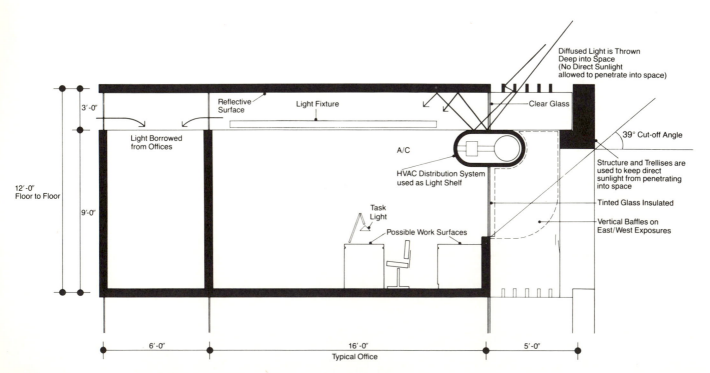

FIGURE 6-31.   A cross section of the developed design of a typical office for the Shell Oil complex.

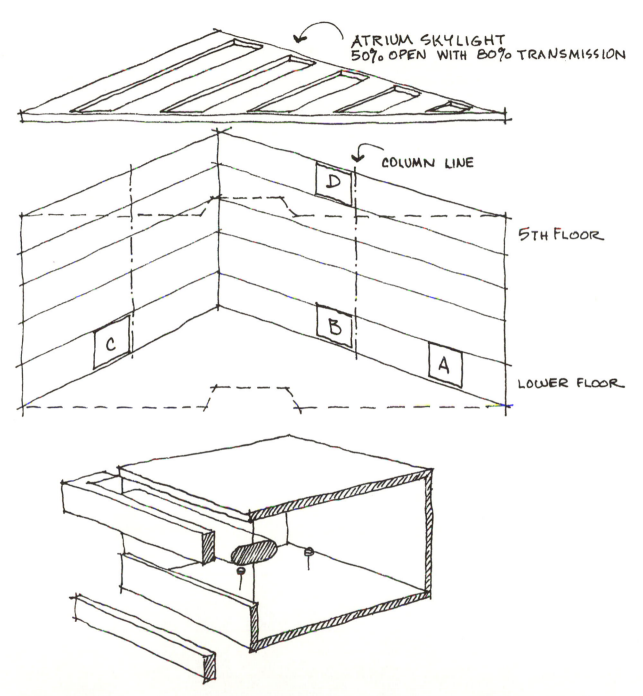

ATRIUM SKYLIGHT
50% OPEN WITH 80% TRANSMISSION

COLUMN LINE

D

5TH FLOOR

C

B

A

LOWER FLOOR

FIGURE 6-32. SCHEMATIC SHOWING ROOM-TEST LOCATIONS IN **MODEL NO. 2** AND CUT-AWAY OF **OFFICE** MODEL MOVED FROM ONE **LOCATION** TO ANOTHER FOR DAYLIGHT **TESTS.**

FIGURE 6-33. Photograph of the inside of the
atrium model.

FIGURE 6-34. Model No. 2 of the atrium being
tested on the CRS parking lot.

## OVERCAST SKY: $E_H = 5,000$ F.C.
### JUNE 1

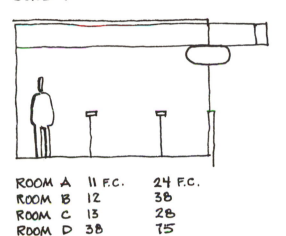

| | | |
|---|---|---|
| ROOM A | 11 F.C. | 24 F.C. |
| ROOM B | 12 | 38 |
| ROOM C | 13 | 28 |
| ROOM D | 38 | 75 |

## CLEAR SKY: $E_H = 9,000$ F.C. (APPROX.)
### JUNE 15

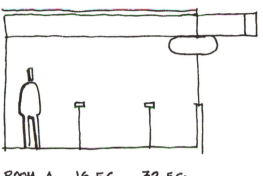

| | | |
|---|---|---|
| ROOM A | 16 F.C. | 32 F.C. |
| ROOM B | 16 | 31 |
| ROOM C | 16 | 34 |
| ROOM D | 64 | 120 |

FIGURE 6-35. Results of tests on Model No. 2 under a clear sky and an overcast sky (see Figure 6-34 for room A,B,C, and D locations).

structed. Removable access panels were cut into the atrium walls so that the office could be moved from one location to another for testing, thus saving model construction time and cost.

This model was tested in Houston on the CRS parking lot. Since only the atrium area with daylight entering through the atrium skylight was of concern, the surrounding landscape was of no significance (i.e., there were no nearby objects to significantly obstruct light from reaching the skylight).

The model was tested under an overcast sky and under a clear sky. The results indicate that on a dark day very little daylight penetrates those offices on the lowest floor facing the atrium (see Figure 6-35). Under such weather conditions, electric lighting would be necessary. Under clear sky conditions, the levels of daylight in the offices were much higher.

**Full-Scale Prototype Study.** Concurrent with the model testing, CRS commissioned the construction of a full-scale pro-

FIGURE 6-36. The author measuring illumination levels in the full-scale prototype. For an exterior view of the model, see Figure 8-4.

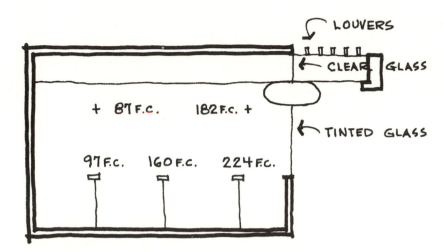

FIGURE 6-37. THE RESULTS OF DAYLIGHT TESTS ON THE PROTOTYPE UNDER A PARTLY CLOUDY SKY.

totype of a single office which could be used primarily for observation, but also for daylight tests. The space was completely finished on the interior and equipped with furniture, electric lights, carpet, books, and even papers on the desk. Subjective impressions by observers, including the clients, indicated that the environment was quite pleasant and the seeing conditions excellent.

The point to be made here is that the model studies were not used as a technique for determining whether or not the design would meet specific quantitative levels (e.g., a specific number of footcandles). The model studies were used by the architects as one of a number of study tools to arrive at a total design which would result in the best possible lighting environment within the given constraints. There is no question that the model studies were a vital part of the process.

# 7

# COST-EFFECTIVE DAYLIGHTING DESIGN

When the energy crunch hit in the early 1970s, it was brought to the attention of the building industry that nearly half the energy consumed in non-residential buildings was for electric lighting. Since the trend at that time called for increasingly high levels of illumination, even to the point of using luminaires as space-heating elements, questions about the value of all that illumination overwhelmed the "scientific" arguments in favor of lots of light. Building owners and operators began removing lamps from luminaires or disconnecting them entirely, in an attempt to save energy through reduced lighting levels.

In 1975, the American Institute of Architects Research Corporation (AIARC), under contract to the Department of Energy (DOE) and the Department of Housing and Urban Development (HUD), began an investigation of current practices in building energy consumption in order to assist in establishing a program of Building Energy Performance Standards (BEPS) as required by Congressional edict. As one effort in that lengthy process, AIARC selected a number of representative buildings across the country designed prior to the energy crunch in 1972 and contracted with the architects to redesign these buildings to be more energy efficient. This effort was an experiment to determine how much energy might have been saved in the original buildings had the designers known what was about to happen to the energy supply and had they understood and applied techniques for energy conservation in building design.

A review of the results of those redesigns for AIARC indicated that, over-all, the designers had quickly focused on the two areas of easiest and most significant design changes to achieve energy savings—adding insulation to walls and roofs and cutting back on the *quantity* of electric lighting. Notice that this says nothing about *quality* of lighting. Most of the designers simply and arbitrarily reduced the design light levels by 50 percent or more. That was a quick and easy way to save a generous portion of energy as well as capital and operating costs. In addition, most of the designers took credit for the energy savings of daylighting from their conventionally designed windows which previously had been considered, by general practice, as "energy losers," with the daylight contribution incidental. Only a few designers made any effort to actually determine how much daylight they could expect from their designs, and the greatest percentage of those efforts were quite unsophisticated.

The point to be made here is that energy *savings* has little meaning unless associated with some type of benefit. The best way to save energy is not to use it! But, of course, we use energy because of the many benefits that are possible from it—benefits such as heat, light, and power. Energy conservation, on the other hand, is using as little of the precious stuff as necessary to achieve those benefits. Therefore, any effort toward determining the costs of building design alternatives must be linked to the *benefits* derived. Energy can be saved by reducing light levels by 50 percent, but this ignores the benefit side of the equation (the benefits received from that level of light). Even more energy could be saved by reducing light levels by 100 percent, but then we couldn't see and the benefits would be completely lost.

It is here that daylighting shows one of its biggest cost advantages. Daylight, because of its directional qualities, will produce fewer veiling reflections for most visual tasks (superior quality lighting) than a typical ceiling-mounted electric lighting system. Since it takes 10 to 15 percent more illumination to make up for each 1 percent loss in contrast, due to veiling reflections, most tasks require two to three times as much illumination from overhead sources as from side-wall lighting. (See Figures 7-1 & 2.) Therefore, the required number of footcandles is only one-third as much for daylighting as for the typical electric lighting system to achieve similar quality.

But cost-effective utilization of daylighting is linked directly to the integration of daylighting consideration into the architect's total design concept. It must be considered from the very beginning in relation to all other design parameters. It is a poor return on investment to bring in the lighting designer after the design concept has already been established.

Analysis of the life-cycle cost-benefit of design alternatives is complicated by the lack of knowledge about many contributing factors, so the designer must make assumptions based on best judgment. In the case of daylighting, for instance, there is very little data on how much daylight is available outside the building. The consideration of available daylight must be based on standard calculation techniques for "typical" sun and sky situations which are somewhat suspect. The only empirical data available is percentage of cloud cover, which is recorded at weather bureau stations by the National Oceanic and Atmospheric Administration (NOAA). Even this data has limited applicability since its measurement is based on an observer's estimate. Such voids in the knowledge of the physical environment leave many uncertainties.

## FIRST COSTS

With the current economic situation and the rapidly increasing costs of building construction, many building clients search for the simplest and least costly building designs. Although the more sophisticated clients are looking at total life cycle costs, first costs are still a major consideration. Many architects assume that good day-

TABLE 7-1.  Effect of light source location on seeing task contrast.

| LOCATION AND TYPE OF LIGHT SOURCE | AVERAGE FOOTCANDLES ON TASK | VIEWING ANGLE (DEGREES) | SEING TASK CONTRAST PENCIL BALL-POINT PRINT (ON WHITE PAPER) | | |
|---|---|---|---|---|---|
| OVERHEAD | | | | | |
| LUMINOUS CEILING | 70 | 30 | 67 | 83 | 78 |
| SIDEWALL | | | | | |
| OVERCAST SKY | 70 | 30 | 89 | 97 | 91 |
| VENETIAN BLIND | 70 | 30 | 85 | 93 | 87 |

lighting design will increase the capital cost investment and have difficulty in convincing their clients and, in many cases, in convincing themselves that designing for daylight will be cost-effective.

If the design concept is confined to the rectangular room with windows on one wall, there is little that can be done to make daylighting effective without adding measurably to the building's first cost, outside of switching or dimming the perimeter electric lights.

However, if the designer includes daylighting as a prime consideration in the total design, allowing daylight to influence spatial relationships, form, and detail, from the very beginning of the design process, the first-cost investments specifically attributable to daylight may be small, and probably difficult to delineate.

In the case of Louis Kahn's Kimbell Art Museum, how can the cost of those elements of the design (e.g., the "daylighting fixture," the glass-enclosed court) that in-

TABLE 7-2.  Task contrast of light sources compared to task contrast with an integrating sphere.

| LIGHTING SYSTEM | ESI | BRIGHTNESS IN GLARE ZONE (FOOTLAMBERTS) | CONTRAST | % LOSS OF CONTRAST |
|---|---|---|---|---|
| INTEGRATING SPHERE | 70 | 70 | 95 | 0 |
| DIFFUSE LUMINAIRE | 25 | 750 | 84 | 11 |
| LOUVERED LUMINAIRE | 15 | 2500 | 60 | 35 |
| SIDEWALL LIGHT SOURCE | 150 | 20 | 104 | -9 |

troduce and control daylight be designated as attributable to daylighting when their costs might be as well attributable to aesthetic quality or total "atmosphere"?

When first-cost investments can be shown to provide sufficient benefits, such as a reduction in energy use over the life of the building, increased quality of lighting conditions, or a more beautiful space, daylight design will be more easily justifiable to the client.

Of course, if daylighting is thought of only in terms of adding controls to a conventional building design, then certainly first costs will be increased (perhaps maintenance costs too) and cost-effectiveness may be difficult or impossible to achieve.

Daylighting is part of the total building cost-benefit picture and should not be treated as an "add-on." The cost-benefit of design for daylighting must be considered in conjunction with other lighting costs and benefits, with solar heat gains and losses, with energy uses and savings, and so forth. There is no simple conclusion about the cost of daylighting that can be applied to all buildings. The analysis of each building must take into consideration the specific circumstances particular to that site and program.

## OPERATING COSTS

The energy and economic savings possible through the use of daylight are realized by the owner over the life of the building and are a result of decisions made by the architect during the design process. It can be anticipated that as energy costs continue to escalate, the use of daylight to supplement or replace electric lighting will become more attractive to clients. But daylighting is not an isolated phenomenon. It is a package deal which includes heat gains and losses and therefore affects energy-intensive heating and air-conditioning (HVAC) systems. It is the relative costs of maintaining the luminous and thermal environments which make up the single largest consideration in cost-effective daylighting design and the area which promises the greatest rewards.

For the past 20 years, windows have been considered by HVAC engineers principally in terms of solar heat gain or con-

ductive and radiant heat loss—solar gains during the air-conditioning season and heat losses during the winter heating season. In each case, the engineer was seeking criteria for determining maximum loads as a basis for sizing mechanical equipment. Although this has little to do with actual energy usage or savings, it has planted in the minds of many the idea that windows are energy losers.

But this process fails to take into consideration that solar heat gain in the *winter* saves on heating energy usage and that by turning electric lights off in warm weather when daylight is sufficient, significant savings can be accrued for both lighting and air-conditioning costs.

Recent studies have shown that when both heat gains and losses associated with windows and skylights are considered over the life of a properly designed building, significant energy savings can accrue. The National Bureau of Standards (NBS) reports that an analysis of a typical residence in the Washington, D.C. area shows that when the costs of heating, cooling, and lighting are taken into account, a properly managed, medium-sized (12- to 60-square-foot) window can affect a present value savings of $1000 over a 25-year period.[1]

In a computer-aided study of a rectangular room with windows on one side for Los Angeles, Jurovics calculated a 46 percent reduction in the annual thermal load when daylighting was considered. With the use of an "optimized" window size, the load reduction was an even greater 53 percent.[2]

Rudoy and Duran have shown that in a study of a 13.5-foot square office with a 9-foot ceiling and windows on one side, the reduction of load on the air-conditioning system that resulted from the lights being turned off, plus the reduction in electric energy used, more than compensated for the increase in winter load on the heating system from the windows.[3] The use of an internal heat recovery system would increase the savings to 17 to 19 million Btu per square foot annually. According to Crisp, a dimming system rather than an on-off photo-electric switching system can save an additional 25 percent in electric lighting energy.[4]

Murdock has developed a procedure for

calculating the potential savings in lighting energy from the use of plastic-dome skylights and has applied this system to the analysis of a hypothetical interior lunchroom at six different locations throughout the United States. The analysis does not include the heat losses and gains due to exterior weather conditions which, of course, would be necessary for a total picture of the heat exchange and energy-saving properties of skylights. Assuming six 4 by 4-foot double-dome skylights (8 percent of the roof area), Murdock found the following data for Oklahoma City:

TABLE 7-3. Lighting Energy Usage in Btu/Yr for a Lunchroom in Oklahoma City[5]

| Cooling Season: | Lights off for an average of 7.75 hr/day |
|---|---|
| Lighting Energy Saved: | 7,390,000 Btu/yr |
| Increase in Cooling System Energy: | 3,042,000 Btu/yr |
| Increase in Heating System Energy: | 1,430,000 Btu/yr |
| Net Energy Savings: | 2,918,000 Btu/yr |

Murdock reports that, of the six locations analyzed, only one showed a slight lighting energy loss. Three showed greater savings than the Oklahoma City site. He concludes that "... properly designed and insulated double-dome skylights usually result in over-all energy savings ..."

Recent work at the Building Research Establishment in England has resulted in the development of a procedure for determining the daylighting savings with either dimming or on-off controls. The procedure begins with the determination of the percentage of time that various daylighting levels will be achieved in the building space under consideration.*

Figure 7-1 shows the number of hours per year that various inside light levels are equaled or exceeded for a ratio of interior (at the task) to exterior daylight (measured on the unobstructed horizontal plane of the ground), assuming that the building in use will require a level of 50 footcandles for 2500 hours during the year. The large rectangle in the diagram is proportional to the total energy consumed with an all-electric lighting system. The example 1:3 daylight ratio line (ratio of indoor to outdoor daylight) intersects the 50 footcandle design illumination level at 1000 hours, indicating that 50 footcandles is exceeded at the indoor point of consideration for 1000 hours of the year. No electric light would be required for this period, but for the remaining 1500 hours electric light would be required. The total savings would thus be 40 percent of the energy needed if electric light were used entirely. For this period, a system with dimmers would also be off, thus effecting no additional savings. However, as the interior light level drops below 50 footcandles, the dimming system would provide just enough light to maintain the 50 footcandle level. For dimmer systems with a linear light power curve, the energy savings are shown by the triangular portion of the diagram. In this example, the dimmer system would save nearly twice as much energy as the simple on-off system.

Pike and Golubov, in a study for the Department of Energy, conclude that "the proper use of daylight-sensitive, photoelectrically-controlled, perimeter lighting is shown to have significant energy and life cycle cost-benefit impact on a typical, new construction office building in the climate of the New York City region."[6] Such controls are said to have a discounted, after-tax payback of under four years. In addition, the source energy used by the base building was reduced by 10 percent, and the peak demand was cut by 9 percent.

One can assume that as the cost of energy increases, more efficient electric lighting systems will reach the marketplace, somewhat offsetting the direct energy savings now possible with the use of daylight. But an even more compelling reason for daylight use rests in the concept of peak power loads.

In most areas of the country, commercial

*Records from the National Oceanic and Atmospheric Administration (NOAA) can provide data on percentage of overcast days, clear days, and partly cloudy days for a number of localities throughout North America. On the basis of this data, the daylight contribution to illumination in the building for each of these conditions can be calculated or determined through model tests.

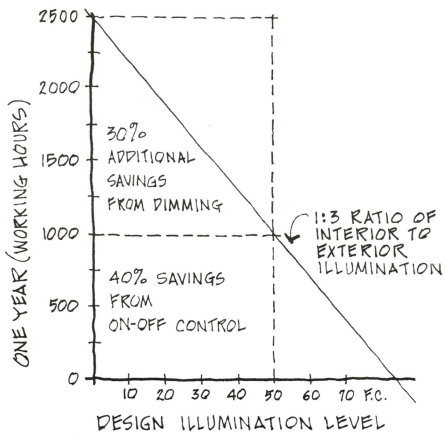

FIGURE 7-1. Energy savings from daylight with on-off electric light controls and dimming controls.

firms pay not only for the quantity of electric energy used, they also pay an additional fee based on their peak demand, which may amount to a significant portion of the firm's total electric bill. Many utilities now implement selective rates through time-of-day policies which penalize use of energy during peak load periods, such as midday in the summer, when air-conditioning demands are greatest. The use of daylight instead of electric light can reduce not only the total energy demand, but it also reduces the peak load demand during the daylight hours.

## BLACKOUT COSTS

Most of the cost considerations already mentioned may be insignificant by comparison to the costs for *not* having daylight when there are power shortages and power failures. The so-called "blackout" has become a common occurrence in many cities throughout the country and, if the experts are correct, we can expect the problem to get worse.

Suppose 2000 persons work for $8 per hour, 8 hours per day, in a 30-story windowless building in a downtown metropolis. If there is a power failure and the employees cannot function in their jobs for lack of light, the employer will lose $16,000 per hour, or $128,000 per day. If a daylong blackout occurs just once a year, in ten years the employer will have lost $1,280,000 in salaries, not to mention losses from failure to complete production tasks on schedule, and from accidents, heart failures, and emotional stresses brought about by the abrupt onset of darkness! Blackouts, from whatever cause, can be significant to overall operating costs.

## DETERMINING LIFE CYCLE COSTS

Life cycle cost-benefit (LCCB) analysis is one concept which allows consideration of the economic consequences of design decisions in terms of money spent today (present cost) and money spent during the life of the structure (annual costs). It especially allows for quick comparison of the cost-benefit ratios of alternative designs, both at the subsystem and total system levels. While direct costs are more easily dealt with, benefits, too, can usually be expressed in terms of financial value. For instance, the long-term benefit of having a large window in an office may be expressed in terms of the higher rental value made possible by the window. The successful application of this concept requires that both costs and benefits be assessed on the basis of a careful delineation of the relevant elements to be included and a method of measurement and evaluation that can appropriately be compared.

LCCB analysis for lighting design is based on the total relative cash flow anticipated over the expected life of the facility for each design alternative. All relative costs and benefits are expressed in current cash value at the time they are expected to occur. These values are then transformed into either an equivalent uniform annual-cost model or an equivalent present-worth model at some opportunity rate which is the interest rate at which the resources of the building owner or client could be invested elsewhere).

The basic theory of LCCB analysis is beyond the scope of this discussion, but two examples of the application of the concept are included in the Appendix. While specific cost figures quickly become obsolete, the techniques used for comparing design alternatives remain valid.

## CONCLUSION

In many economic analyses, little consideration is given to the benefit side of the equation, the *quality* of the lighting produced. It is often assumed that if daylight reaches the task or target area, the electric lights can be turned off and energy saved. Similarily, consideration of the *quality* of electric lighting is often ignored. This detracts from the meaningfulness of the analyses and leaves it to the reader to make judgments as to the benefits related to the design schemes compared, which brings us full circle to where we started: that good daylighting design can save energy and improve lighting quality, but each case must be considered individually, and all of the related considerations of thermal loads, structural integrity, and spatial quality must be part of the evaluation.

# DESIGNS WITH DAYLIGHT: CASE STUDIES

It is the exception rather than the rule to find recent buildings designed principally around daylight. Though most buildings built in the last 30 years have included a substantial portion of glass, the glass was used more for view and visual integration of spaces than for daylight. Most designers intuitively use glass to let a little daylight into corners, room perimeters, and corridors, with the result that sometimes their glassed-in spaces are quite successful and sometimes dismal failures. When asked to explain their objectives with regard to daylight, only a few designers exhibit an understanding of the basic principles of good visibility and good daylighting design.

During the past ten years, the concept of the central shopping mall and hotel atrium has caught on significantly. Hardly a city today does not have at least one prime example of such a space. Designers have discovered that people like the excitement of the large, open space and the changing patterns of daylight and sunlight. From the standpoint of visibility—veiling reflections, brightness relationships, glare, etc.—the spaces are large enough and flexible enough so that a person can move around to avoid discomfort. But in most cases, the designers abandoned any concern with daylight when the remainder of the building was conceived. The result is a scattering of isolated instances in which daylight has been used excellently in some portions of buildings and poorly in most other portions.

Up to this point, the basic principles of good daylighting design have been discussed and illustrated with sketches and photographs of selected parts of buildings. In this chapter, several buildings may be seen from a broader context to gain an understanding of how the entire design process can be approached with daylight in mind. All should serve to indicate that designing with daylight can and does produce beautiful as well as functional buildings which satisfy some of humankind's longing for kinship with the sun and weather and which inspire and uplift daily living.

FIGURE 8-1. Perspective of the Shell Oil Company Woodcreek Exploration and Production Offices.

Courtesy of Caudill Rowlett and Scott

## SIDELIGHTING
Buildings in which daylight comes principally from the side.

**Shell Oil Company Woodcreek Exploration and Production Office, Houston, Texas.** Caudill Rowlett Scott, architects/planners/engineers; project director, James Gatton, AIA; design principal, Charles Lawrence, FAIA; senior project designer, Rey de la Reza; Benjamin H. Evans, AIA, daylighting consultant; Jules G. Horton, lighting consultant; Michael Sizemore, energy consultant.

Programmatic requirements, a cooperative client, and an architectural firm with a long history of interest in environmental factors made the use of daylight in the new Shell buildings a natural happening. The key element which stimulated the daylight approach was Shell's requirement for a maximum number of private offices with outside views in an energy-conscious and efficient complex.

The requirement for numerous individual offices normally calls for a long narrow building design with a central circulation corridor and offices on either side. To avoid the inefficiencies of such a strung-out design, CRS's idea was to stack the offices into a multistory building and to fold the long, narrow wings around a central, triangular-shaped atrium which would reduce the exposed perimeter wall areas by nearly half. A precast concrete framing system that extends beyond the office spaces to the outdoors was developed which provided opportunity for sun shading and bouncing the daylight into interior spaces.

To further enhance the daylight contribution and to achieve significant economies, a perimeter HVAC system was developed that would extend half inside and half outside the plane of the window glass, acting as a light shelf to bounce daylight into interior areas. This design eliminated the need for a hung ceiling, allowing an increase in effective floor-to-ceiling height. The window wall utilizes clear glass above the HVAC light shelf and tinted glass, intended primarily to provide a view out, below the HVAC shelf.

The precast-concrete, double-T structural floor and ceiling provided not only for

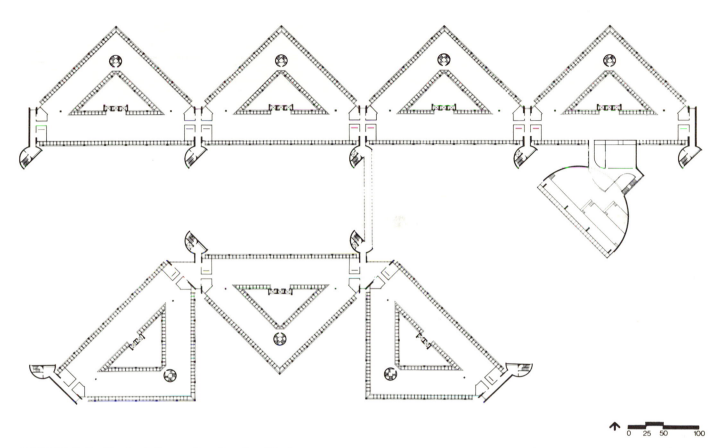

FIGURE 8-2. Typical floor plan for the Shell Building.

daylight entry at the window wall, but also for a suspended, indirect, fluorescent, luminaire system. The two systems blend together unobtrusively when used simultaneously without producing significant veiling reflections below.

Independent switching of the electric lights and individual desk task lamps allow each office occupant a choice of lighting options to suit individual needs—a demand from Shell to avoid any inconvenience to the highly productive occupants.

Some of the offices face to the exterior of the beautifully wooded Houston site, and some face into the skylighted central atrium. All offices were to be lighted principally with daylight with the expectation that the electric lights would be used only rarely. The model studies described in Chapter 6 were undertaken to determine the parameters of the atrium skylight necessary to provide adequate daylight for those offices on the atrium.

At this writing, the Shell complex is still under construction, so it is not possible to evaluate the results of the total design. But the daylight conditions in the full-scale prototype were near perfect even under an overcast, rainy sky, providing a very pleasant and functional lighting environment. The electric lighting energy consumption has been estimated at 0.87 watts per square foot of floor space based on a conservative projection of annual use.

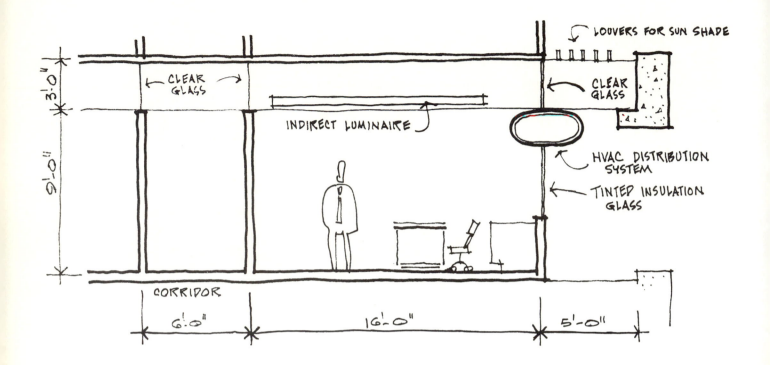

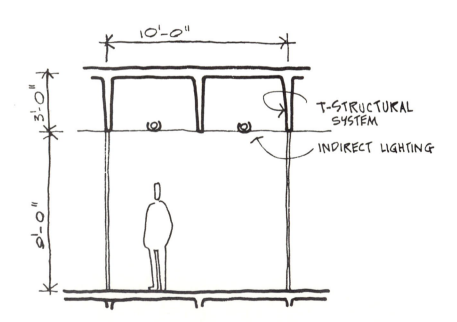

# FIGURE 8-3. CROSS SECTIONS THROUGH A TYPICAL OFFICE SPACE.

FIGURE 8-4. The full-scale prototype of a typical Shell office.

FIGURE 8-5. The author inside the Shell prototype during a rainstorm—daylighting only.

FIGURE 8-6. Splayed jambs and exterior planting filter and soften the daylighting in this delightful residence.

**The Rotunda, University of Virginia, Charlottesville, Virginia.** Thomas Jefferson, architect.

The library building at the University of Virginia, designed by Thomas Jefferson with assistance from Benjamin Latrobe, was modeled after the exterior of the Roman Pantheon, which had its own unique daylighting characteristics. While Jefferson's Rotunda is not a hollow shell like the Pantheon, attention to the admission of daylight is just as admirable and much more suited to the quiet academic atmosphere of the Virginia hillsides.

The library study rooms use splayed window jambs to soften surface contrasts (see Figures 8–6 and 8–7) and light-colored surfaces to reflect and diffuse the daylight. This reception area at the foot of the stairwell (see Figure 8–8) shows how beautifully and softly the daylight from the upper-floor areas bounces down the stairs to provide excellent and pleasant seeing conditions. The few electric lights seen in this photo contribute very little to the ambient lighting.

FIGURE 8-7. This sitting room has a nice quality of daylight.

FIGURE 8-8.   Even at the foot of this stairwell, the daylighting is even and sufficient for desk work.

**Angela Athletic Facility, St. Mary's College, South Bend, Indiana.** C.F. Murphy Associates, architects.

This facility uses daylight extensively in the indoor recreation areas, bringing the light through clear 1/4-inch acrylic curved panels around the perimeter window walls and skylights. Additional daylight enters the building through perimeter 2 1/2-inch translucent panels made of inner and outer fiberglass sheets with insulation in between.

Direct sun frequently penetrates the clear acrylic panels and produces bright areas on the gym floor, but also satisfies the biological need for contact with the exterior environment.

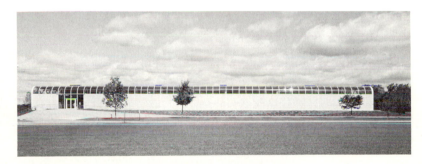

FIGURE 8-9.   The Angela Athletic Facility at St. Mary's College with its curved acrylic daylight panels.

FIGURE 8-10. The interior is well lighted, although overly generous quantities of direct sun frequently light areas of the gym floor. The translucent fiberglass wall panels could produce excessive brightness contrasts for some athletic activities.

FIGURE 8-11. The curved, clear acrylic panels allow biological connection with the exterior as well as generous quantities of daylight. The translucent wall panels have low transmission characteristics but are good thermal insulators.

## SKYLIGHTING

Buildings in which daylight comes principally from skylights overhead.

**Montrose Elementary School, Laredo,
Texas.** Caudill Rowlett Scott, architects;
A.A. Leyendecker, Associates, associate
architects; Benjamin H. Evans, AIA, daylighting consultant.

This low-budget school was designed
and built in 1959 for the hot Texas-Mexican
border climate where the sun shines almost 100 percent of the daylight hours. The
sun shining on the flat soil which has almost
no permanent vegetation creates an excessive brightness condition which led
to the development of this quadruplex
scheme that turns in on itself to provide a
shaded view out of the classrooms to the
central recreation areas.

Daylight for the classrooms enters
through roof-mounted plastic dome skylights and through the window wall shaded
by an outdoor translucent fiberglass-
reinforced plastic canopy with a 20 percent
light transmission factor. Glare through the
windows is controlled by judiciously placed
wood screens and a specially treated non-
reflective pavement.

After developing the basic design
scheme, the architects needed answers
about the number, size, and type of skylights to use and the desirable transmission characteristics of the outdoor play
canopy. Two model tests were conducted
for the designers by the Texas Engineering
Experiment Station at Texas A & M College,
the first using skylights and the second with
the outdoor canopy. The results are shown
here.

The model studies indicated a more than
ample supply of daylight (more than 100
footcandles most of the daylight hours)
with three skylights for each classroom
and the contribution of the side windows
under the canopy. There was little concern
for conditions of the relatively rare overcast
sky. In the final design, eggcrate louvers
were substituted for the plastic ceiling panels under the skylights to further reduce
visible brightness. The model tests also indicated that a canopy with a transmission
factor of about 16 percent would be about
right. The material finally bid on and accepted for the canopy cover had a rated
transmission factor of 20 percent.

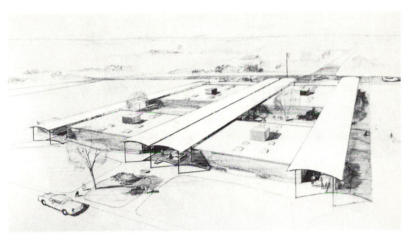

FIGURE 8-12. Perspective of the Montrose Elementary School.

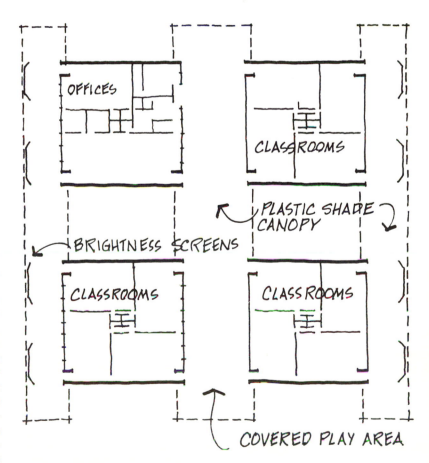

FIGURE 8-13. FLOOR PLAN OF
THE MONTROSE SCHOOL

FIGURE 8-14. The outdoor shade and brightness control canopy.
Photo: Roland Chatham

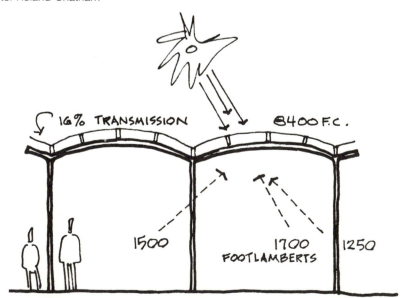

FIGURE 8-15. CANOPY BRIGHTNESS
TEST RESULTS.

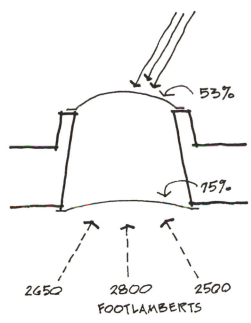

FIGURE 8-16. SKYLIGHT
BRIGHTNESS TEST
RESULTS.

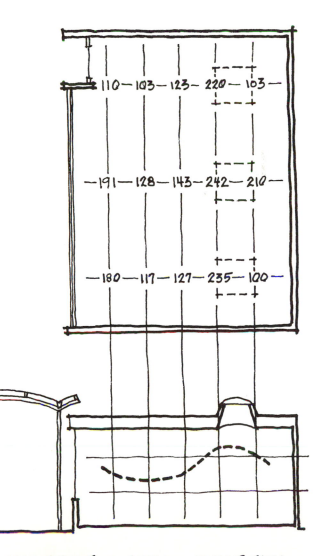

MONTROSE SCHOOL – CLEAR SKY:
$E_V$ =  860 F.C.
$E_H$ =  2150 F.C.
$E_{HS}$ = 8700 F.C.

FIGURE 8-17.  CLEAR-DAY MODEL TEST
RESULTS FOR A **TYPICAL** CLASSROOM.

**Kimbell Art Museum, Fort Worth, Texas.** Louis I. Kahn, architect; Richard Kelly, lighting consultant.

Undoubtedly, the Kimbell Art Museum is one of the finest and most beautifully daylighted buildings in the world. It should rank among the classics of all times. Louis Kahn has been called the "poet of lighting" because of his sensitivity to the value of daylight in building design and the Kimbell Art Museum is the epitome of all in daylighting design that is good.

Daylight in art museums has historically been approached with much fear and trepidation because of the deterioration that can result, in paintings particularly, from the ultraviolet in daylight. Kahn elected to use daylight at its softest level for ambient lighting in the Kimbell Art Museum on the assumption that the deterioration would be nonexistent or, at least, very minimal. He expected his daylight to satisfy biological needs, "... giving the comforting feeling of knowing the time of day" and of providing "... as many moods as there are moments in time. ..."[1]

The museum is constructed of a series of adjoining cycloid concrete vaults 100 feet long and 23 feet wide with a clear skylight continuous along each vault ridge. The incoming daylight is bounced and filtered by the "natural lighting fixture" suspended just below the skylight. The shape of the concrete vault and curve of the daylight fixture were selected through computer analysis to provide the appropriate reflection and diffusion of daylight. The daylight fixture consists of a frame on which is attached metal sheeting, punched with enough tiny holes to allow some daylight penetration to modify any possible sharp contrast between the underside of the fixture and the adjacent daylighted concrete vault. The precise details of the sheeting configuration were determined only after four successive experimental models were

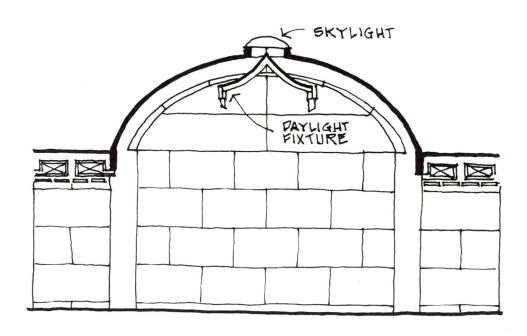

FIGURE 8-18. KIMBELL ART MUSEUM
CROSS SECTION OF A TYPICAL BAY.

FIGURE 8-19.  The Kimbell Art Museum.

FIGURE 8-20.  The entrance area. Note the Yu-pon trees trimmed to form an umbrella of shade that provides a visual transition from the bright exterior to the less severe interior.

FIGURE 8-21.  Entrance area.

FIGURE 8-22. View from lobby down corridor, stairwell (through doorway).

FIGURE 8-23. North Court and refreshment area.

FIGURE 8-24. Typical gallery.

Courtesy of Kimbell Art Museum, Fort Worth, Texas

studied in place during construction. In certain locations, the central portion of the sheeting on the daylight fixtures was left opaque to block direct sun.

Slits of clear glass were used between the structural and non-structural parts of the vaults and framing system as the "beginning of ornament," and also to bring in daylight, providing some direct contact with the outside.

Contact with the direct exterior is also provided by the interior courts which Kahn said were ". . . named for the kind of light that I anticipate their proportions, their foliation, or their sky reflections on surfaces or on water will give."[1] The courts were planted with delicate elm trees trimmed to grow along the wire struts over the courtyard area, thus filtering the daylight as it flows into the court and building.

The exterior daylight illumination level under a variable overcast sky was measured at about 1200 footcandles on a recent summer overcast day. Inside, the level was 12 to 15 footcandles on the floor under the concrete vaults. On one of the display tables, the illumination level measured 30 footcandles. With the normally bright Texas sun shining, the levels would be substantially higher. In the library—the one functional area which seems somewhat cramped—the lighting level on the table top was over 80 footcandles with the fluorescent lights burning. In general, the electric lights in the museum blend well with the daylight, highlighting displays and exhibit areas without being obtrusive. The total lighting environment inside the Kimbell Art Museum is entirely pleasant, with varying degrees of interest but without harsh surprises.

FIGURE 8-25.   Fountain Court.

FIGURE 8-26.   Library.

FIGURE 8-27. North Court and delicate elm growth for filtering daylight.

FIGURE 8-28. The natural lighting fixture of perforated metal.

FIGURE 8-29. The entrance area and outdoor shade vault.

**Alfred C. Glassell, Jr. School of Art, Houston, Texas.** S.I. Morris Associates, architects.

A very unique building, the Glassell School of Art employs clear glass block for the exterior walls and prismatic glass block for the skylight over the central court. The clear glass block provides a semi-obscured view to the exterior, where objects are just barely perceptible, and allows daylight and some direct sun to penetrate into the building. Students working in the building indicated to me that the general lighting was very pleasant. The prismatic glass block over the court area provides ample quantities of daylight without direct sun penetration. The transmission of the block is low enough to avoid excessive brightness normally, and the skylight is large enough to allow sufficient daylight. The clear glass walls at the ends of the court area allow some view of the bright Houston sky, but because of the location they do not significantly interfere with visibility of exhibits in the court.

FIGURE 8-30. The glass-block-clad Glassell School of Art.
Photo: Rick Gardner

FIGURE 8-31.   The clear glass block allows ample daylight to enter with a semi-obscured view of the exterior.

FIGURE 8-32.   A prismatic glass-block skylight daylights the central court.

FIGURE 8-33.   An interesting design feature is the enlarging lens stuck on the clear glass walls of the court near the stairs.

**Academic Building, University of Petroleum and Minerals, Dhahan, Saudi Arabia.** Caudill Rowlett Scott, architects/planners/engineers; Benjamin H. Evans, AIA, daylighting consultant.

A cross section of the preliminary design of the Academic Building for the University of Petroleum and Minerals is shown here. Daylight was intended for ambient light during typical clear sky conditions. Model tests were used to determine the size of the skylights and the skylight (translucent) transmission factor needed to allow a minimum of 30 footcandles in most areas of both floor levels.

A typical section through the building was selected for testing. A model was constructed at a scale of 1:20. The light-reflecting characteristics of the walls, floors, columns, and ceiling surfaces were duplicated in the model with appropriate paints. There were no significant textural considerations. Glass areas in interior offices were simulated with gray paint having a 25 percent reflectance. (Glass reflects some of the incident light, but allows most to pass through.)

The model included only a section of the total area of the building. For testing, this area had to be completely enclosed to prevent the penetration of unwanted light. These enclosing walls, along the lateral sides of the model, were painted to achieve 25 percent reflectance to simulate the light lost into these almost infinite open areas of the building. (Some of the skylight is lost into these open areas and some is received from other areas. The assumption here that more light is lost than received is a conservative one.) In all respects, the dimensions and details of other items of the spaces were duplicated relatively closely.

The skylights in the model were constructed at scale with a 1.2-meter diameter opening and covered on top with a flat translucent plastic having a transmission of 49 percent. This flat material does not exactly duplicate a vacuum-formed plastic dome skylight, but is sufficiently close.

The tests were conducted in the country-side of Blacksburg, Virginia, which can hardly be equated with Saudi Arabia. However, since only skylights were to be considered (no light from side windows) the nature of the surrounding landscape is irrelevant. All incident light is from the sky and sun (no reflected ground light reaches the skylights). To approximate the Saudi sun and sky, which has been estimated to produce an illumination of 12,000 footcandles on the horizontal plane of the roof, a multiplication factor is applied to the light levels measured in the model. Different glazing transmissions can be approximated using multiplication factors. Thus, it is possible to simulate a number of conditions using the data measured in the model under one set of conditions. The process isn't strictly accurate, but the margin of error is small.

The results of the daylight tests are shown in Figure 8–35:

Column 1 provides the light levels measured with the basic model (skylight diameter = 1.2 meters; skylight glazing transmission = 49 percent) with an illumination from sun and sky on the horizontal roof ($Eh$) of 6000 footcandles.

Column 2 indicates calculated light levels in the model for a roof plane illumination level of 12,000 footcandles, approximating the Saudi Arabia sky.

Column 3 indicates calculated light levels to be expected with a smaller diameter skylight.

Column 4 indicates calculated light levels expected with the smaller skylight opening and a lower skylight transmission factor of 69 percent.

Other combinations of skylight opening and transmission factor can be studied using the same basic measurement data. A skylight transmission factor of 30 percent, for instance, can be simulated by multiplying the figures in Column 3 by a factor of 30/49. A skylight diameter of, say, 0.8 meters can be simulated by multiplying the numbers in Column 3 by a factor of 0.8/1.0.

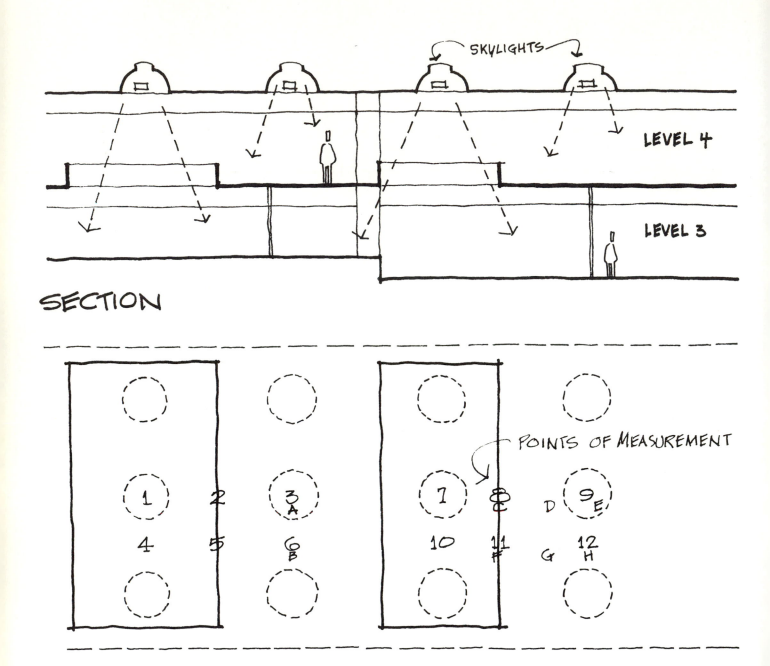

SECTION

PLAN (NOT TO SCALE)

FIGURE 8-34. CROSS SECTION AND FLOOR PLAN (NOT TO SCALE) INDICATING THE LOCATIONS OF POINTS AT WHICH THE ILLUMINATION MEASUREMENTS SHOWN IN 8-35 WERE TAKEN.

# DAYLIGHT TEST RESULTS — UNIV. of P. & M.

11:20 A.M. SOLAR TIME — OCT. 29
41° TRUE SUN ALTITUDE
13°E SUN AZIMUTH

| POSITION | 1 MEASURED $E_h$ = 6,600 d = 1.2m t = 49% | 2 CALCULATED $E_h$ = 12,000 d = 1.2m t = 49% | 3 CALCULATED $E_h$ = 12,000 d = 1.0m t = 49% | 4 CALCULATED $E_h$ = 12,000 d = 1.0m t = 69% |
|---|---|---|---|---|
| 1 | 14.3 | 26.1 | 18 | 25 |
| 2 | 12.7 | 23.2 | 16 | 23 |
| 3 | 5.8 | 10.5 | 7 | 9 |
| 4 | 20.5 | 37.3 | 26 | 37 |
| 5 | 17.2 | 31.2 | 22 | 31 |
| 6 | 6.9 | 12.5 | 9 | 13 |
| 7 | 9.6 | 17.4 | 12 | 17 |
| 8 | 8.8 | 15.9 | 11 | 15 |
| 9 | 2.9 | 5.2 | 4 | 6 |
| 10 | 16.7 | 30.2 | 21 | 30 |
| 11 | 14.1 | 25.5 | 18 | 25 |
| 12 | 3.6 | 6.5 | 5 | 7 |
| A | 30.1 | 54.3 | 38 | 54 |
| B | 39.5 | 71.2 | 49 | 69 |
| C | 33.6 | 60.5 | 42 | 59 |
| D | 30.1 | 54.2 | 38 | 54 |
| E | 15.6 | 28.1 | 20 | 28 |
| F | 27.7 | 49.8 | 35 | 49 |
| G | 36.9 | 66.5 | 46 | 65 |
| H | 8.7 | 15.7 | 11 | 15 |

LEVEL 3 (positions 1–12)
LEVEL 4 (positions A–H)

$E_h$ = ILLUMINATION ON HORIZ. ROOF
d = DIAMETER OF SKYLIGHT
t = TRANSMISSION FACTOR OF SKYLIGHT

FIGURE 8-35. Shown in Column 1 are footcandle measurements in the model with an exterior illumination level from sun and sky of 6600 footcandles. Column 2 shows footcandle levels as a result of mathematically transposing the figures in Column 1 to a sky with a 12,000 footcandle level as expected in Saudi Arabia. Columns 3 and 4 give footcandle levels calculated on the basis of Column 1 for different skylight diameters and transmissions.

FIGURE 8-36.   The model at the test site. The interiors of the skylight "domes" were modeled to scale, but the exterior of the domes shown here was rough and thick to facilitate fabrication.

FIGURE 8-37.   The model being prepared for clear-sky tests.

**Chapel at Massachusetts Institute of Technology, Cambridge, Massachusetts.** Eero Saarinen, architect.

Saarinen's chapel at MIT is an excellent example of daylight used for drama. This daylighted chapel focuses attention on the altar and background sculpture, which are dramatically lighted by a large overhead skylight. Patterns of daylight are reflected from the pond of water surrounding the exterior up into the interior and onto the undulating circular walls (not shown in these photographs). The eye adapts to the transition from the bright exterior to the subdued interior of the chapel through means of the translucent walled entrance area.

FIGURE 8-38.   The MIT Chapel by Eero Saarinen.
Courtesy Massachusetts Institute of Technology, Cambridge, Massachusetts

FIGURE 8-39.   The skylight dramatically highlights the altar and background sculpture.

FIGURE 8-40.   The entrance area provides for eye adaptation and transition from the brightly lighted exterior to the subdued interior.

FIGURE 8-41. The four-story entrance area of the Yale Center for British Art.

**Yale Center for British Art, New Haven, Connecticut.** Louis I. Kahn, architect.

This building on the Yale campus is another of Louis Kahn's daylight-sensitive designs, though not as totally devoted to daylighting as his Kimbell Art Museum. The four-story Center building is based on a rectangular structural grid, pierced at various levels with wells, or atria, which are topped with skylights. A number of the top floor spaces are also lighted with skylights, while some of the lower spaces borrow daylight from the skylighted walls. Each skylighted bay is covered by four plastic-dome skylights which are shaded above the roof by louvers to prevent direct sun penetration. These louvers are positioned so as to bounce an increased amount of daylight into the building when the sun is

FIGURE 8-42. Paintings are softly daylighted by the plastic-dome skylights.

low in the sky and a reduced amount when the sun is high—moderating the changing quantities. Below each skylight is a sandwich of clear plastic, egg-crate louvers, and a patterned plastic lens.

The subdued daylighting through the skylights on an overcast day makes electric lighting most often unnecessary. This amount of daylighting control is probably overly sophisticated for the results achieved, but proponents of the design might argue otherwise.

The deep, slanted concrete structural members which support the roof and skylights help to soften contrasts between the skylights and surrounding surfaces. The soft texture of the stone walls allows the daylight to be diffusely reflected without gloss.

FIGURE 8-43. Galleries on the top floor are lighted by skylights.

FIGURE 8-44. Some of the top-floor galleries also borrow daylight from the adjacent skylighted atria.

FIGURE 8-45. The plastic-dome skylights are shielded from direct sun by roof-top louvers and direct view of the skylights from below by a patterned plastic ceiling panel.

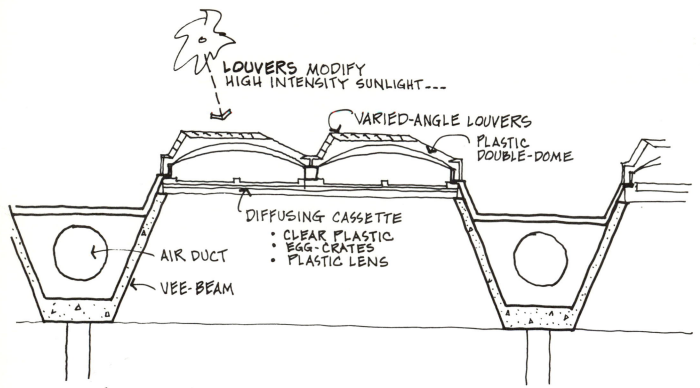

LOUVERS MODIFY
HIGH INTENSITY SUNLIGHT...

VARIED-ANGLE LOUVERS

PLASTIC
DOUBLE-DOME

DIFFUSING CASSETTE
• CLEAR PLASTIC
• EGG-CRATES
• PLASTIC LENS

AIR DUCT

VEE-BEAM

FIGURE 8-46. EXTERIOR LOUVERS, MOUNTED OVER THE SKYLIGHTS, MODIFY THE HIGH-ANGLE SUNLIGHT, BUT ALLOW PLENTY OF LOW-ANGLE DAYLIGHT INTO THE INTERIOR.
YALE CENTER FOR BRITISH ART – LOUIS I. KAHN

FIGURE 8-47.   The rooftop skylights shielded by metal louvers.

## CLERESTORIES
Buildings in which the daylight comes principally from vertical openings in the roof.

**Dallas City Hall, Dallas, Texas.** I.M. Pei & Partners and Harper & Kemp, architects.

From the standpoint of daylighting, Pei created a truly magnificent "great court" in his Dallas City Hall, where the citizens of Dallas come into contact with their day-to-day government. The court, seven stories in height, is topped with three continuous, parallel clerestory vaults. The court is the principal public space and was obviously intended to be seen and experienced. It forms a very pleasant and cool atmosphere, providing relief from the bright Texas exterior and summer heat.

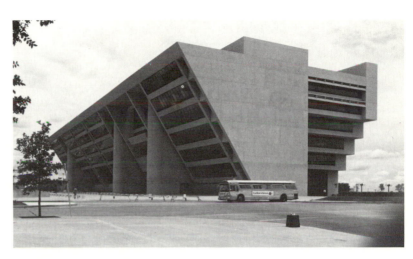

FIGURE 8-48. The Dallas City Hall.

FIGURE 8-49. The seven-story high public space court.
Photo: Robert Lautman

FIGURE 8-50.   The court and one of its clerestories showing the stepped floor areas below.

The vaults are beautifully formed to admit the north light and reflected sunlight, providing ample quantities of interior daylighting. Unfortunately, the building's sensitivity to daylight is not carried into other areas. Offices next to the court area borrow some daylight, but the electric lights have to burn anyway'

Typical work spaces extend inward from the sloping glass exterior walls from which they receive daylight. The interior areas are dimly lighted even with the recessed downlights burning. Employees are oriented so that they face parallel to or away from the windows to avoid the harsh contrasts created by the brightly lighted exterior. Some of the perimeter office areas are nicely daylighted, but wherever there is a view to the bright exterior, contrasts are extreme. All exterior glass is slightly tinted.

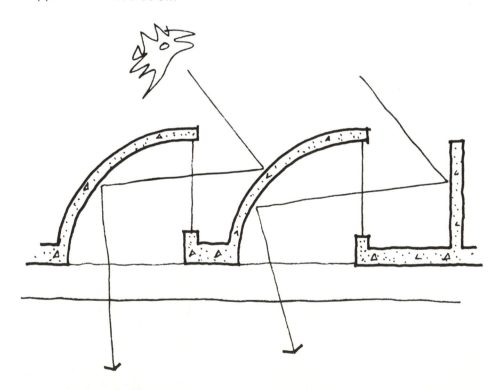

# FIGURE 8-51.  CROSS SECTION THROUGH THE CLERESTORIES.

FIGURE 8-52. The clerestories as seen from below and the offices which borrow daylight.

FIGURE 8-53. Typical office space with high ceiling and electric downlights.

**George Gund Hall, Harvard Graduate School of Design, Cambridge, Massachusetts.** John Andrews, Architects.

Gund Hall seems to be a very controversial building—there are proponents and opponents to the type of environment created inside. Without getting into questions of appropriateness of the whole building, these photographs illustrate some points about daylight control worth considering.

The building's prime space is the gigantic studio area where design students toil over their drawing boards from sunrise to sunset, intermingling with faculty and other students. The studio space consists of five stepped levels, sometimes referred to as trays, overlapping one another and covered with a long span of alternating clerestories and roof slabs, which are oriented, generally, toward the east.

While sun control for some areas for some periods of the day is non-existent, generally the daylighting of the space is surprisingly good. Many of the students supplement the daylight with task lamps on their desks, but this is not necessarily an in-

FIGURE 8-54. Gund Hall as viewed from the south.

FIGURE 8-55. The stepped studio space.

dication that the daylighting scheme is poor. The photograph here illustrates how the clerestories allow daylight while the roof slabs restrict view of the sky brightness. Where trees can be viewed through the clear glass clerestories, visibility is pleasant. Where the sky can be viewed directly, the brightness relationships are less than desirable.

Note, however, in these photographs, that the translucent covering over the long-span trusses creates an excessively bright area when compared to the view through the clerestories. In this situation, the translucent material over the trusses is, perhaps, more desirable than would be an opaque material, but something with transparency would have been even better if the technology (and budget) had been up to it.

FIGURE 8-56. The clerestories with exposed trusses and mechanical equipment.

FIGURE 8-57. A lounge area adjacent to the studio space.

**Huntington Gallery Addition, Huntington, West Virginia.** The Architects Collaborative, architects.

This addition to the Huntington Gallery uses clerestories and windows to supplement electric lighting of the objects of art. The clerestories are glazed with translucent panels and shielded on the interior by operable vertical louvers. Daylight bounces around the curved back of the clerestory area to light the wall below, but because of the vertical directional qualities of the daylight, electric lights must be used also on the art itself.

FIGURE 8-58. The translucent panels of the clerestories allow daylight to enter the curved-vault areas.

FIGURE 8-59. The clerestory translucent glazing is shielded on the inside by operable vertical louvers.

FIGURE 8-60. Daylight from the clerestory washes the upper portions of the wall and provides general ambient lighting.

FIGURE 8-61.  The East Building of the National Gallery of Art in Washington, D.C.

## ATRIA
Buildings in which daylight comes from a large, central skylighted atrium.

**East Building, National Gallery of Art, Washington, D.C.** I.M. Pei & Partners, architects.

Pei's East Building is often referred to as an "event" or an "experience" as much as an art gallery. In large part, this has to do with the design of the "great courtyard" again. In contrast to his Dallas City Hall, this court is much more open in terms of both space and daylight. In the East Building, the

FIGURE 8-62.  The triangular skylights over the cafeteria area which lies under the pavement near the entrance to the East Building.

emphasis is on excitement and wonder, whereas the emphasis in the Dallas City Hall design is on peace, calm, and cool.

Daylight is admitted to the grand court, almost uninterrupted, by the huge, heavy, steel-framed skylight laced with delicate aluminum sunscreening. Numerous streaks of sunlight penetrate the screening, apparently set in a random pattern, lending a constant and rapidly changing atmosphere of light in the court. Very few works of art are displayed in the court, so the emphasis is on circulation and grandeur rather than visibility. The more serious works of art are displayed in small galleries around the perimeter, some lighted with electric light only, and some with skylights over a translucent, suspended ceiling.

FIGURE 8-63. The great courtyard and large skylights with aluminum sunscreen.

FIGURE 8-64. The entrance, mezzanine, and grand court areas.

FIGURE 8-65.  The Anotole Hotel atrium-lobby.

**Anatole Hotel, World Trade Center, Dallas, Texas.** Beran & Shelmire, architects.
This hotel has two quite large undivided atrium spaces, in contrast to many of the Regency Hotels in which the atrium spaces tend to be divided by elevator shafts, escalators, stairs, etc. Each of the Anatole atriums is capped by a large, steel-framed, transparent skylight which allows ample supplies of both sun and skylight to enter. In spite of this daylight, electric lights burn constantly, presumably to add emphasis and focus to interior areas.

FIGURE 8-66.  Daylighting at the ground floor of the atrium is filtered by the general space as well as by plantings and awnings around the central cafe.

**Crown Center Hotel, Kansas City, Missouri.** Harry Weese & Associates, architects.

This hotel was built on an existing hill of rock which has been left intact to provide a dramatic atrium-lobby, capped with a clear glass skylight and surrounded by glass walls and clerestories. The general level of daylight is more than ample, but because the vegetation and rocks throughout the space are visually interesting, occupants are almost required to look up, and, hence, their eyes take in areas where the brightness contrast between interior and exterior as viewed through the glass walls is often uncomfortable.

FIGURE 8-67. The hotel was built on a hill of rocks, which provides the focal point for the large hotel atrium-lobby.

FIGURE 8-68. The existing rockpile which extends up several stories from the second floor of the lobby.

FIGURE 8-69. The mezzanine glass walls and clerestory.

FIGURE 8-70. Clear-glass skylights flood corner areas of Crown Center with daylight.

**Detroit Plaza Hotel, Detroit, Michigan.**
John Portman and Associates, architects.
The atrium-lobby space here is divided by a proliferation of building components which bounce and filter the daylight from the multilevel clear glass skylights. Day- light provides general ambient lighting with highlights of direct sun bounced and filtered by the building components and vegetation. Brightness contrasts tend to be overemphasized in the photographs.

FIGURE 8-71. The Detroit Plaza clad in mirrored-glass walls.

FIGURE 8-72. The lobby-atrium space, where ambient daylight is combined with electric lights for highlights.

FIGURE 8-73. The atrium clear-glass skylight.

FIGURE 8-74. Atrium columns and circulation components bounce and redirect daylight; trees filter it.

## LUMINOUS STRUCTURES

Buildings which admit daylight through translucent or transparent building skins.

**Thomas E. Leavey Activities Center and Harold J. Toso Pavilion, University of Santa Clara, Santa Clara, California.** Caudill Rowlett Scott, architects/planners/engineers; Albert A. Hoover & Associates, associated architects.

The air-supported, cable-restrained structure is a somewhat unique type of facility, but it has special daylighting characteristics. This facility uses a translucent Teflon-coated fiberglass skin with steel restraining cables for a cover and top. The cover is supported by an environmental control system that maintains a 5-psf pressure differential between inside and outside.

The cover allows an ample supply of daylight into the interior so that electric lights are unnecessary during most days and allows enough ultraviolet for a healthy growth of vegetation. The brightness of the cover is sufficiently subdued so that harsh contrasts are not created, yet it provides an excellent background against which the range and speed of flying balls are easily perceived.

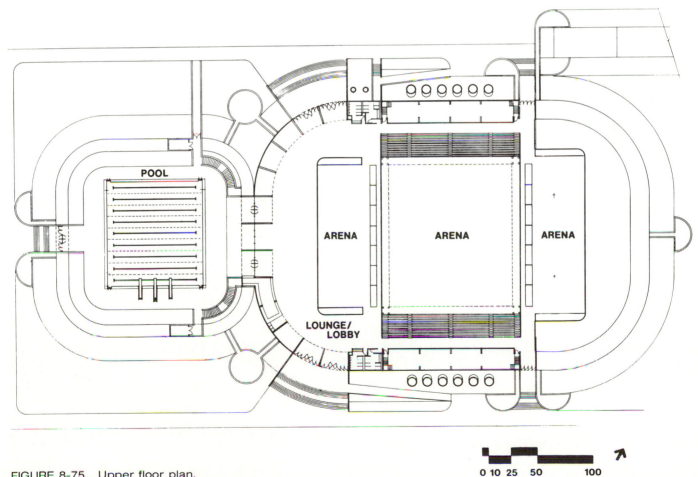

FIGURE 8-75. Upper floor plan.

0 10 25 50      100

FIGURE 8-76. The retractable cover over the pool (foreground, left) and the permanent cover over the activity center (background).
Photo: Julius Shulman

FIGURE 8-77. Volleyball players in the activity center.
Photo: Balthazar Korab

FIGURE 8-78. The cover provides enough daylight and ultraviolet light to support vegetation.
Photo: Balthazar Korab

FIGURE 8-79. Daylighting is uniformly distrib-
uted, but varies over the day—participants still
have a sense of contact with the outdoors.
Photo: Julius Shulman

FIGURE 8-80. The differing visual aspects of the exterior of the cathedral depend upon the direction from which one approaches and the reflections of light, sky, and adjacent buildings on its angled roof and wall planes.

Photos and captions: Robert E. Fischer

## The Crystal Cathedral, Garden Grove Community Church, Garden Grove, California. Johnson/Burgee Architects.

Perhaps one of the most dramatic and unusual buildings of this century, the Crystal Cathedral demonstrates all of the daylight design guidelines put forth in Chapter 4. In this glass-enclosed church, daylight is used to achieve a variety of moods and to maintain a truly meaningful relationship with the outdoor natural environment.

The building envelope consists of 1/4 inch and 3/8 inch panels of "silver" coated glass. The coating reduces the transmission of light by 82 percent and radiant heat by 80 percent, but is transparent and allows clear vision from inside to outside, providing "biological" contact with nature. From the outside, the coated glass tends to appear as a bluish mirror picking up reflections of surrounding areas. The structure which supports the glass envelope consists of white-painted pipe trusses carefully designed to give a lattice-like appearance, effectively "filtering" the incoming daylight and avoiding any perception of excessive brightnesses.

Daylight is brought in high in the structure, as well as through the lower areas, and is "bounced" off the floor and other surfaces. It is the extensive use of the coated glass which enables ample amounts of daylight to enter the space, even through the 8 percent transmission glass. Such glass used in more typical quantities would not provide much daylight. The building is oriented so that the sun enters predominately from behind the seated congregation, thus reducing the chances for glare which might interfere with good vision.

The design provides excellent integration of daylight and other environmental concerns. Cooling is provided by natural air movement through operable glass panels and doors. There is no mechanical cooling system. Thermal air currents are allowed to exit through upper windows to carry off warmed air. The solar heat contribution supports the winter-time warm air heating system, but is slight enough not to cause overheating in summer. The thickness of the glass panels is varied to suit acoustical demands without detracting from the daylighting scheme.

FIGURE 8-81.   The quality of pearly light which suffuses the interior whether the sky is overcast or clear can better be seen in the color photo on the jacket. The structure is a rhythmic series of space trusses formed by pipe members painted white.

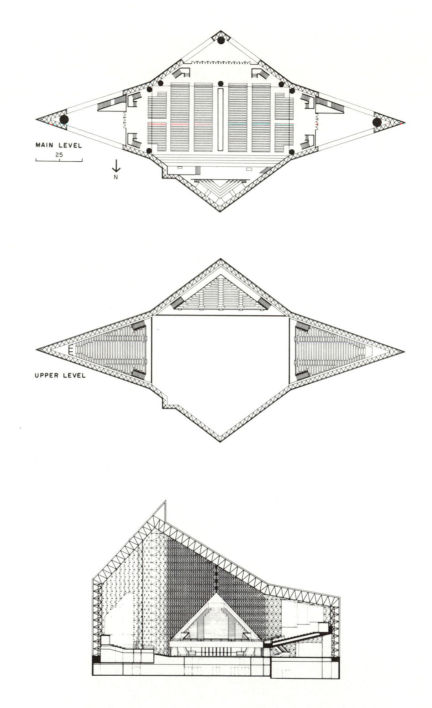

MAIN LEVEL
25
N

UPPER LEVEL

FIGURE 8-82.   The building is 415 feet long, 207 feet wide, and 128 feet high at the apex. As this section and the floor plans detail, the building achieves intimacy through skillful sculpturing of space and a "pinched" diamond plan that pulls all the congregants in as close as possible to the altar.

Photos and captions: Robert E. Fischer

FIGURE 8-83.   The Crystal Cathedral is not air-conditioned. Operating windows in the walls and the peak of the roof cool the building by providing cross ventilation.

# APPENDIX

# LIFE CYCLE COST BENEFIT ANALYSIS

## Example 1:

The following is taken from Kirk[1] as an example of life cycle cost analysis as it is practiced by the Detroit architectural and engineering firm of Smith, Hinchman & Grylls Associates. The LCCB technique is illustrated by this case study of a seven-story office facility.

The location and exposure of the office areas (north and east) and the client's goal of energy conservation strongly suggested various combinations of daylighting schemes and supplemental lighting systems.

The several issues to be examined in depth included: a) fenestration; b) artificial lighting; c) energy conservation; d) mechanical requirements; e) direct versus indirect lighting; f) coffered versus flat ceiling; and g) lighting reflective devices.

Using brainstorming techniques, the team developed a number of daylighting schemes appropriate to the facility, and a number of artificial lighting systems for comparison. From these lists, four daylighting schemes were selected for evaluation. Sections of these schemes are represented in Figure 1. The original daylighting scheme comprised two 4-foot-high windows in an aluminum curtain wall. The ceiling was coffered to allow natural light-

ing to penetrate the space to a greater degree, and a reflective louver was positioned on the exterior wall to decrease glare and focus the natural light.

Three daylighting alternatives were compared to the original in terms of both life-cycle costs and other important criteria. The first alternative was a conventional office design with a coffered ceiling and one 6-foot-high window. The second alternative was similar to the original design (i.e., two 4-foot windows and a coffered ceiling), but lacked the reflective louvers and surfaces.

The final daylighting alternate consisted of a recessed, single, 4-foot-high window, slightly sloped; a reflective ceiling panel; and a 9-foot ceiling height.

Four supplemental lighting systems capable of attaining an ambient level of 50 footcandles were selected for comparison with the schemes: a fluorescent, parabolic three-tube, direct, 2- by 4-foot fixture; a fluorescent, two-tube, indirect 6-inch by 4-foot fixture; a high-pressure sodium, 250-watt fixture capable of being dimmed; and an HPS 250-watt fixture with switching capability.

The interaction of the daylighting schemes with the various supplemental lighting means produced 16 possible solutions for evaluation. Criteria and their corresponding weighted importance were established as follows:

Life cycle cost estimates were prepared next for the various daylighting and lighting fixture alternates. Figure 2 is an example of the completed estimate for the four daylighting schemes using a high-pressure sodium fixture with switching capability. Supplemental lighting energy requirements were estimated from daylighting data provided by the computer analysis program LUMEN 2. (This program was developed by Smith, Hinchman & Grylls to analyze lighting system performance.) A computer analysis also determined the cooling energy requirements of the alternate configurations.

Maintenance costs were estimated for window washing, re-lamping, minor repair and cleaning; costs for replacement of venetian blinds, lighting fixtures, etc. were also included. The daylighting scheme with reflective louvers had the advantage of supplying an investment tax credit. The HPS fixture is considered by the Internal Revenue Service as "furniture" and, as such, may be depreciated over a seven-year period rather than over the building life of 40 years. The "credit" also has been assigned. Because the exterior wall design of Alternative 3 created less usable space for the client, it was assessed an "associated" cost. This denial of use (space) cost estimate was based on similar office space rental in the area. Finally, a 10 percent salvage value (credit) was given to each daylighting scheme.

Each annual life cycle cost was converted to "present worth" (based on a 10 percent interest rate and a 40-year economic life) using a discount table. One-time costs of replacements were also converted to present worth. The summation of initial, operational, maintenance, replacement, tax-related, associated, and salvage pres-

ent-worth values becomes the life-cycle cost for each alternate.

Once the life-cycle costs were established for each of the 16 combinations, these schemes were given "points" in the weighted evaluation. Figure 3 is a summary matrix of these alternates. The total point score of each is presented first, and the lower portions of each box contain the estimated present-worth costs. The recommended solution—the one with the highest composite score—was a combination of daylighting alternates 1 and 2. A 2-foot-high upper window and a 4-foot-high lower window with a coffered ceiling was suggested to the client as was the high-pressure sodium fixture.

Until recently, only initial cost dollars have been of prime concern in the building cycle. However, life cycle costing techniques offer the opportunity to impose limits by the owner of thresholds for the designer to achieve, making the establishment of energy budgets, maintenance targets, and other ownership and operational constraints possible. As experience grows in these areas, more efficient performance can be expected in the operation of buildings.

The best opportunity for saving life cycle dollars is in the earliest stages of the design process. As previously discussed, the concepts, for the most part, are well established. Difficulty may come in actually integrating them in developing facilities that meet owner requirements at a lower total cost of ownership. Owners must take the responsibility for setting realistic goals in the planning/budgeting phase, requiring LCC, and providing funding as necessary to A/E's so that life cycle costing doesn't become just another paperwork exercise. A typical project ranging from $4 to 6 million requires approximately 400 to 600 additional manhours of effort to adequately review the significant areas.

## Example 2:

This example of life cycle cost analysis from Wenzler[2] provides a comparison of costs for two different lighting schemes and for an office with two different orientations. Since the price of electric energy has

increased so dramatically since these figures were developed, the life cycle cost picture would be even more favorable to daylighting in today's marketplace.

The office furniture and work areas are

oriented in such a manner that reflected glare is negligible. The office space is 30 feet long and 20 feet wide with a ceiling height of 10 feet. The ceiling is white and the walls have a 50 percent reflectance. The office tasks require 70 to 100 footcandles, five days a week or approximately 2500 hours per year. The office is located at 40° north latitude and has 120 overcast days per year. The daylight source is a window wall 30 feet long and 7 feet from the ceiling to the sill. Adjustable venetian blinds cover the entire window area. The fluorescent unit is a 4–40-watt, rapid-start commercial luminaire with 45- by 45-degree louvers.

The cost per footcandle is used to compare the economics of the various sources. To establish this criterion for each alternate, it is necessary to compute the number of units required and the illumination they provide. This is accomplished by using the lumen method of artificial lighting prediction for the electric alternate,[3] and the lumen method of daylight prediction for the daylight alternate.[4]

Seventeen fluorescent fixtures are required to provide a minimum of 70 footcandles on the working areas, from electric lights only.

The amount of daylight in any office varies with exterior conditions. It is, therefore, necessary to compute the distribution of daylight in the office for the minimum exterior sky conditions. The distribution of daylight in the office is assumed to be 192 footcandles near the window, 97 in the center, and 56 near the inner wall, if the exterior condition is an overcast sky of 1000 footlamberts and the ground has an average reflectance of 20 percent. This condition represents one of the low values of daylighting in the room, and the process described earlier of basing the daylight contribution on percent cloud cover would show the economic results would be even more favorable to daylighting. The average illumination from daylighting can, if desired, exceed 100 footcandles, or it can diminish by closing the blinds. However, for economic comparison the daylight will be assumed to be 70 footcandles.

A step-by-step economic analysis of these two types of lighting schemes is

TABLE A-1. Economic Analysis for Integrated Lighting (Electric Lights Used Only 1000 hours)

| Type of Lighting | Fluorescent | Daylight |
|---|---|---|
| 1. Distribution | Direct-Indirect | Direct-Indirect |
| 2. Control | 45 × 45° louvers | Venetian blinds |
| 3. Source | 4-40-watt warm white, rapid start | Overcast (minimum conditions) |
| 4. Electric watts | 184 | 0 |
| 5. Number of units | 17 | 30 × 7 ft window |
| 6. Footcandle design illumination | 70 | 0 (low average for minimum conditions) |
| 7. First cost installed | $1,215.00 | $527 differential compared to typical masonry wall |
| 8. Uniform annual cost of recovering first cost | $ 80.75 | $ 35.03 |
| 9. Annual cost of insurance | $ 36.45 | $ 15.81 |
| 10. Annual cost of property tax | $ 36.45 | $ 15.81 |
| 11. Annual cost of electric energy | $ 78.20 | 0 |
| 12. Annual cost of lamps or blinds | $ 15.26 | $ 24.93 |
| 13. Annual cost of maintenance | $ 8.50 | $ 12.60 |
| 14. Total annual cost | $ 255.61 | $104.18 |
| 15. Annual cost [per fc] | $ 3.65 | $ 1.49 |

shown in Table A-1. The electric lighting system will operate for 2500 hours per year in one case, and 1000 hours in the second case when daylight is used. The first seven items of Table A-1 are self-explanatory. Item 7 is the first cost of each alternate installed. The electric alternate includes the cost of the luminaires and $10 installation cost per unit, which is a conservative figure. The differential cost of 50 percent operable windows, as opposed to a typical block and brick wall, is used as the first cost of daylight. The actual differential of $2.51 per square foot is a very conservative figure.

Item 8 is the uniform annual cost of re-

TABLE A-2. Summary of Economic Analysis for Lighting an Office

| Lighting Source | Illumination | Uniform Annual | |
|---|---|---|---|
| Fluorescent | 70 fc | $395.81 | $5,955 |
| Daylight | 70 fc | $104.18 | $1,568 |
| Daylight and Fluorescent (1000 hours) | 70 fc Daylight 30 fc Fluorescent 100 fc Total | $104.18 $109.50 $213.68 | $3,215 |

TABLE A-3. Economic Thermal Analysis of Two 30 × 20-Foot Offices, One Oriented East and One West

| Type of Lighting | 70 fc Daylight 30 fc Fluorescent Standard Lamps | 100 fc Fluorescent Standard Lamps (no daylight) |
|---|---|---|
| 1. Heat gain Btu/hr Window or masonry wall Artificial lighting Maximum | 25,704 10,048 25,704 | 672 30,144 30,816 |
| 2. Tons of A/C to remove maximum heat gain at design conditions | 2.23 | 2.57 |
| 3. Total first cost for extra A/C | $1,561.00 | $1,799.00 |
| 4. Uniform annual cost of capital recovery, 20 yr @ 6% interest | $ 136.08 | $ 156.83 |
| 5. Uniform annual cost of taxes & insurance, 6% of first cost | $ 93.66 | $ 107.94 |
| 6. Annual energy cost for extra A/C | $ 74.76 | $ 100.40 |
| 7. Uniform annual maintenance cost $5/ton of extra A/C | $ 11.15 | $ 12.85 |
| 8. Total uniform annual cost of A/C due to lighting | $ 306.39 | $ 378.02 |
| 9. Uniform annual cost of heat loss through windows or masonry wall | $ 56.95 | $ 10.08 |
| 10. Uniform annual savings in heating due to electric lighting load | $ 7.03 | $ 10.08 |
| 11. Comparative uniform annual cost due to heating and cooling | $ 356.31 | $ 378.02 |

covering the first cost, with interest at 6 percent and a useful life of 40 years. This is probably too long a life for luminaires. Replacement of the luminaires in 20 years would favor daylighting. Item 9 is the annual cost of insurance based on a 3 percent rate of first cost. Item 10 is the annual property tax based on a rate of 3 percent of first cost.

In Item 11, the annual cost of electric energy is based on 2500 and 1000 hours of operation at $0.025 per kilowatt hour. Item 12, the uniform annual cost of replacing blinds or lamps, is based on a 7500-hour life for fluorescent lamps and a five-year life for the venetian blinds. Interest is 6 percent.

Item 13 represents the annual cost of maintenance, and includes the cost of cleaning each alternate once a year. The assumed cost is $0.50 per electric unit and $0.06 per square foot of window area for daylighting.

Item 14 is the total annual cost, or the sum of Items 9–14. Item 15 is the annual cost per footcandle for each alternate, or the total annual cost divided by the illumination.

It is quite obvious that the cost for the daylighting system is considerably less than that for fluorescent lighting alone. Had the first cost of each system been the basis for the decision as to which alternative to use, it would have resulted in a costly mistake.

Table A-2 shows a summary of the annual costs and their present worth, covering 40 years of service. These are not net costs, since no figure has been shown for depreciation allowances, which should be proportionate for each system and are not needed for comparison of alternates.

Thus far, the economic analysis has been based on lighting alone. Where there is light there is heat, and this may be a factor in the over-all economy of the various alternatives. If the building is to be air conditioned, the extra refrigeration as well as heating must be considered.

The two offices considered in Table A-3, one facing east and the other facing west, have the same characteristics used in the previous study. The summer design temperature is 95° F outside and 80° F inside. The winter design temperature is −5° F. The number of heating degree-days is

5000. The equivalent full-load operating hours for air conditioning is 1000 in the daylighted design and 1250 for the artificial lighting with no daylight. Artificial lights are assumed to be used 300 hours during cooling periods and 700 hours during heating periods, with integrated lighting. The peak heating load is computed at 4 P.M. on July 23 using regular plate glass and venetian blinds adjusted at a 45-degree angle. The cost of an extra ton of air conditioning to overcome natural and artificial lighting loads is assumed to be $700. Heating costs are assumed to be $1 per 1000 pounds of steam at 1000 Btu per pound. Air-conditioning operating costs are based on the use of 1.25 kilowatts per ton.

The heat loads and losses for the various combinations are computed using standard techniques. These are shown in Table A-3 with the economic analysis. The cost analysis of a 100 footcandle fluorescent installation using deluxe lamps has been included in this table.

Table A-4 is a summary of the total comparative annual costs and presents relative values of various lighting systems.

It is quite obvious that economic analysis of the over-all design of lighting is necessary for satisfactory results. Any air-conditioning analysis based on heat load of daylighting without the economic comparisons of equivalent electric lighting costs is worthless both to the building owner and architect.

In the daylighting cost analysis, no reduction has been included for the economic advantage gained from having an office more desirable because of windows. This advantage can be estimated on the basis of higher rent charged for an office with window walls, as opposed to one without windows.

Each building owner has a separate rate of return and tax position. Each locale has its particular tax and insurance rates, as well as its own electric rate and daylight conditions. These vary enough to require an economic cost analysis for each different building design. Any attempt to generalize on an economic analysis may prove very costly.

TABLE A-4. Summary of Net Costs for Thermal and Luminous Cost for Two Typical Office Designs

| Lighting Source | Illumination | Uniform Annual Cost of Illumination | Comparative Uniform Annual Cost of Heating/Cooling | Total Comparative Uniform Annual Cost of Illumination, Heating/Cooling | Present Worth of 40 Years of Service (@ 6% Interest) |
|---|---|---|---|---|---|
| Daylight and Standard Fluorescent | 70 fc Daylight 30 fc Fluorescent | | | | |
| | 100 fc Total | $ 427 | $356 | $ 784 | $11,791 |
| Fluorescent Only (Standard Lamps) | 100 Ft-c | $1,130 | $378 | $1,508 | $22,690 |

# REFERENCES

CHAPTER 1

(none)

CHAPTER 2

1. Hopkinson, R.G., and Kay, J.D., **The Lighting of Buildings,** Praeger, New York, 1960.

2. **Performance Criteria: Lighting,** Preliminary Report prepared by the Pratt Institute for the State University Construction Fund, State of New York, October 1965.

3. Lam, W.C.M., **Perception and Lighting as Formgivers for Architecture,** McGraw-Hill, New York, 1977.

4. Flynn, J.E., "The IES Approach to Recommendations Regarding Levels of Illumination," **Lighting Design and Application,** September 1979.

5. Bissonnette, T.H., and Csech, A.G., "Modified Sexual Photoperiodicity in Cottontail Rabbits," **Biology Bulletin,** December 1939.

6. Wurtman, R.J., "Effects of Light and Visual Stimuli on Endocrine Function," **Neuroendocrinology,** *Vol. 2,* 1967.

7. Ott, J., "Effects of Wavelengths of Light on Physiological Functions of Plants and Animals," **Illuminating Engineering,** April 1967.

8. Birren, F., **Light, Color and Environment,** VanNostrand Reinhold, New York, 1969.

9. Richards, S.J., "Sunlight and Buildings," **South African Architectural Record, 52,** No. 12, 1967.

10. Morgan, C.J., "Sunlight and Its Effect on Human Behavior and Performance," **Proceedings of the CIE,** Bouwcentrum, Rotterdam, 1967.

11. Ne'eman, E. and Longmore, J., "Physical Aspects of Windows: Integration of Daylight with Artificial Light," **Proceedings of CIE,** Bouwcentrum, Rotterdam, October 1973.

12. Ruys, "Windowless Offices," (M.A. Thesis, University of Washington, Seattle, 1970).

13. Sommer, R., **Personal Space; The Behavioral Basis of Design,** Prentice-Hall, Inc., Englewood Cliffs, New Jersey, 1969.

14. Wells, B.W.P., "Subjective Responses to the Lighting Installation in a Modern Office Building and their Design Implications," **Building Science, 1,** 1965.

15. Wilson, L.M., "Intensive Care Delirium; The Effect of Outside Deprivation in a Windowless Unit," **Archives of Internal Medicine, 130,** 1972.

16. Pritchard, D., "A Review of Industrial Lighting in Windowless Factories," **Light and Lighting,** 1964.

17. Hollkister, F.D., Greater London Council; **A Report on Problems of Windowless Environments,** Hobbs the Printers, Ltd., London, 1968.

18. Marcus, T.A., "The Function of Windows: A Reappraisal," **Building Science, 2,** 1967.

19. Ludlow, A.M., "The Broad Classification of the Visual Scene: A Preliminary Study, **Vision and Lighting,** Report No. 3, (GIB) November 1972.

20. Keighley, E.C., "Visual Requirements and Reduced Fenestration in Offices—A Study of Multiple Apertures and Window Areas," **Journal of Building Science, 8,** 1973.

21. Hurvich, L.M., and Jameson, D., **The Perception of Brightness and Darkness,** Allyn and Bacon, Boston, 1966.

22. Lam, W.C.M., **Perception and Lighting as Formgivers for Architecture,** McGraw-Hill, New York, 1977.

23. Kruithof, A.A., "Tubular Fluorescent Lamps," **Philips Technical Review,** Eindhoven, Holland, March 1941.

CHAPTER 3

1. Birren, F., **Light, Color, and Environment,** VanNostrand Reinhold, New York, 1969.

2. Evans, B.H., **Natural Air Flow Around Buildings,** Research Report No. 59, Texas Engineering Experiment Station, College Station, Texas, March 1957.

3. Evans, B.H., "Energy Conservation with Natu-

ral Air Flow Through Windows," **ASHRAE Transactions 1979, Vol. 85,** Part 2, 1979.

4. Reed, R.H., "Design for Natural Ventilation In Hot Humid Weather," **Housing and Building in Hot-Humid and Hot-Dry Climates,** National Research Council, 1953.

5. Holleman, T.R., **Air Flow Through Conventional Window Openings,** Research Report No. 33, Texas Engineering Experiment Station, College Station, Texas, November, 1951.

6. Marcus, T.A., "The Function of Buildings: A Reappraisal," **Building Science,** 2, 1967.

## CHAPTER 4

1. Caudill, W.W., and Reed, B.H., **Geometry of Classrooms as Related to Natural Lighting and Natural Ventilation,** Research Report No. 36, Texas Engineering Experiment Station, College Station, Texas, July 1952; Vezey, E.E., Reed, B.H., and Evans, B.H., "Daylight Survey Methods," **Illuminating Engineering,** May 1954.

2. Evans, B.H., "Natural Lighting and Skylights," (M. Arch Thesis, Texas A. & M. College, May 1961).

3. Murdock, J.B., "A Procedure for Calculating the Potential Savings in Lighting Energy from the Use of Skylights," **Journal of the IES,** July 1977.

## CHAPTER 5

1. Kingsbury, H.F., Anderson, H.H., and Bizzano, V.V., "Availability of Daylight," **Illuminating Engineering,** February 1957; Boyd, R.A., "Daylight Availability," **Illuminating Engineering, Vol. 53,** No. 6, June 1958.

2. **How to Predict Interior Illumination,** Libbey-Owens-Ford Company, 1976.

3. **Climatic Atlas of the United States,** U.S. Department of Commerce, Environmental Sciences Services Administration, June 1968.

4. **Climatology of the U.S.** No. 60–44, Climates of the U.S., Government Printing Office, 1970.

## CHAPTER 6

1. Moon, Parry, and Spencer, Domina, **Lighting Design,** Addison-Wesley Press, Cambridge, Mass., 1948.

2. O'Brien, P.F., "Interreflections in Rooms by a Network Method," **Journal of the Optical Society of America,** June 1955.

3. DiLaura, D.L., "On Calculating the Effects of Daylighting in Interior Spaces," **Journal of the IES,** October 1978.

4. Farrell, R., "The Use of the Perspective Techniques in the Calculation of Illumination Levels for Clear Skies," **Journal of the IES,** January 1974.

5. **Recommended Practice of Daylighting,** Illuminating Engineering Society, August 1962.

6. Griffith, J.W., Arner, W.J., and Conover, E.W., "A Modified Lumen Method for Daylighting Design," **Illuminating Engineering,** March 1955.

7. Vezey, E.E., **The Feasibility of Using Models for Predetermining Natural Lighting,** Research Report No. 21, The Texas Engineering Experiment Station, 1951; Reed, B.H., and Nowak, M.A., "Accuracy of Daylight Predictions by Means of Models Under an Artificial Sky," **Illuminating Engineering,** July 1955; Vezey, E.E., and Evans, B.H., "The Study of Natural Illumination by Means of Models Under an Artificial Sky," **Illuminating Engineering,** August 1955.

8. Walsh, J.W.T., **The Science of Daylight,** Pitman Publishing Corp., London, 1961.

9. Weibel, W.A., "Portable Electric Photometers—A Survey," **Lighting Design and Application,** August 1975.

10. Reed, B.H., "Effects of Nearby Walks and Concrete Areas on Indoor Natural Lighting," **Illuminating Engineering,** July 1956.

## CHAPTER 7

1. Collins, B.L., Ruegg, R.T., Chapman, R., and Kusuda, T., **A New Look at Windows,** Center for Building Technology, National Bureau of Standards, January 1978.

2. Jurovics, S.A., "Solar Radiation Data, Natural Lighting, and Building Energy Minimization," **ASHRAE Transactions 1979, Vol. 85,** Part 2.

3. Rudoy, W. and Duran, F., "Effect of Building Envelope Parameters on Heating/Cooling Load and Energy," Dept. of Mechanical Engineering, Univ. of Pittsburgh (unpublished).

4. Crisp, V.H.C., "Energy Conservation in Buildings—A Preliminary Study of the Use of Automatic Daylight Control of Artificial Lighting," Building Research Establishment, England, August 1976 (unpublished).

5. Murdoch, J.B., "A Procedure for Calculating the Potential Energy Savings in Lighting Energy from the Use of Skylights," **Journal of the IES,** July 1977.

6. Pike, T. and Golubov, M., "Cost-Benefit Analysis of Solar Design Alternatives: New Office Building, Temperate Climate," The Ehrenkrantz Group under contract to PRC Energy Analysis Company for the U.S. Department of Energy (unpublished report).

## CHAPTER 8

1. Johnson, Nell E. (compiler), **Light is the Theme: Louis I. Kahn and the Kimbell Art Museum,** Comments on Architecture by Louis Kahn, Kimbell Art Foundation, Fort Worth, Texas, 1975.

APPENDIX

1. Kirk, Stephen J., "Life Cycle Costing, Taken Step by Step," **Architectural Record,** January 1980.

2. Wenzler, O.F., "Present Worth Method: An Economic Analysis of Integrated Lighting," Publication No. 1002, Building Research Institute, Inc., 1962.

3. "Lighting Calculations," Section 9, **IES Lighting Handbook,** Fifth Edition, Illuminating Engineering Society of North America, New York, 1972.

4. **Recommended Practice of Daylighting,** Illuminating Engineering Society of North America, New York, 1979.

# INDEX